908/00

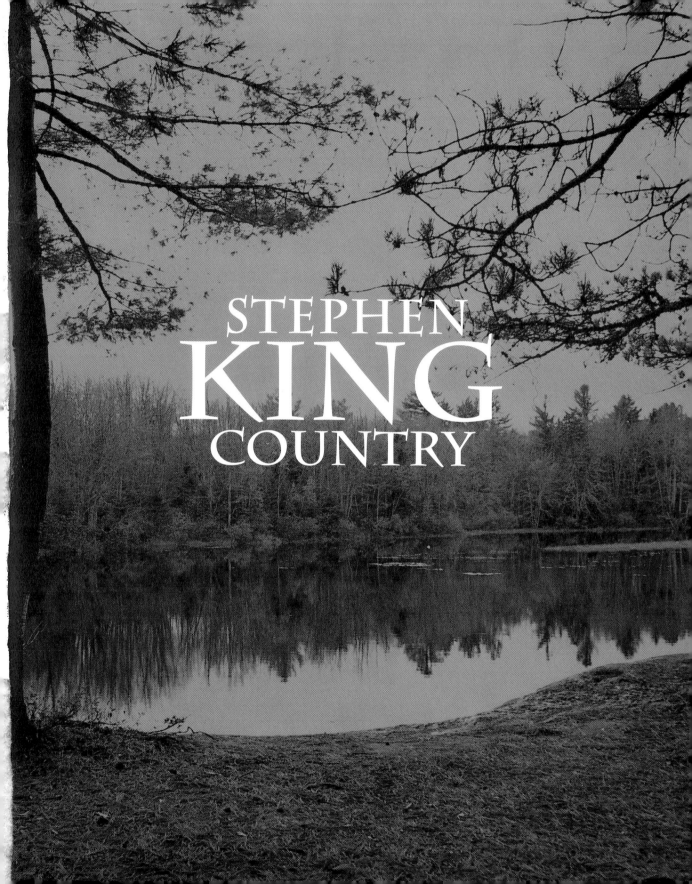

STEPHEN KING COUNTRY

I write about Maine because it's what I know best, but I also write about Maine because it's the place I love best. . . . You have to spend a lot of time in a place before you start to catch the beat of the people's voices, their dialects, and the way they live.

—Stephen King, on Simon & Schuster's website to promote *Bag of Bones* (published September 1998)

STEPHEN KING COUNTRY

BY GEORGE BEAHM

THE ILLUSTRATED GUIDE TO THE SITES AND SIGHTS
THAT INSPIRED THE MODERN MASTER OF HORROR
BY THE AUTHOR OF *THE STEPHEN KING COMPANION*

RUNNING PRESS
PHILADELPHIA · LONDON

9 8 7 6 5 4 3 2 1
Digit on the right indicates the number of this printing

Library of Congress Cataloging-in-Publication Number 98-66652

ISBN 0-7624-0456-6

Photo credits: Unless otherwise indicated, © 1998 by George Beahm.
Photos credited to the *Bangor Daily News* and
Estes Park Trail-Gazette are reprinted with permission.

Cover photo by George Beahm
Typography: Charlemagne, Goudy, Futura, and Nuptial Script

This book may be ordered by mail from the publisher.
Please include $2.50 for postage and handling.
But try your bookstore first!

Running Press Book Publishers
125 South Twenty-second Street
Philadelphia, Pennsylvania 19103-4399

Visit us on the web!
www.runningpress.com

*For Penney and Stuart Tinker, with
friendship well seasoned over the years.*

CONTENTS

Maine is far and away better for a couple of hicks like us.

—Stephen King, in "King of Horror," *Time* magazine (Oct. 6, 1986)

W hen "Maine" is mentioned, the Kodak moments that come into focus are
typically images of picturesque fishing villages dotting the coast or quaint
eateries and inns that cater to the summer people who swell the state's
population by the millions from May until September. Such images are the visual main-
stays of *Down East* magazine, *Yankee* magazine, the many publications of the Maine
Tourism Bureau, and the literature handed out by the local civic organizations. The
goal is to sell you on the state, on Maine as "Vacationland" (it says so right on its
license plate), as "The Way Life Should Be" (the slogan of the Maine Tourism Bureau).

But in *this* book, you won't find any such Kodak moments, because it covers Stephen
King country, on and off the map, on and off the beaten path.

Stephen King's Maine—as opposed to the visual enticements of the Maine Tourism
Bureau—is a view of Maine most tourists never see: places in its southern region like
Center Lovell, Bridgton, Durham, Lisbon Falls, and places like Bangor—the Queen
city—and her surrounding environs, like Hermon, Hampden, Orrington, and Orono.

But to get to the dark heart of Stephen King's Maine, you have to go into uncharted territory—terror incognita, off the edges of the known universe. While there are side trips to places like Rock and Roll, Oregon; Desperation, Nevada; Gatlin, Nebraska; and to a peculiar, haunted hotel high up in the Colorado Rockies, most of Stephen King's fictional world is set in Maine.

Ever heard of Haven, Maine? The Tommyknockers lived there for eons, until they were discovered and began exerting their otherworldly influence on the townsfolk.

What about Chamberlain, Maine? A teenage girl named Carrie nearly burned down the whole town after being humiliated at her prom.

Surely you've heard of 'Salem's Lot—Jerusalem's Lot, which was over-run by vampires some years back, until a fire burned them all out . . . but they're still running loose, stalking their prey.

While you're at it, give Tarker's Mill a wide berth. The werewolf that came to afflict the town is dead—you'd never believe who in town was transformed from man to beast—but there are other things out there that go bump in the night, and they have ravenous appetites and sharp teeth.

Then there's Castle Rock, Maine, where Joe Camber's dog, Cujo, turned rabid after a bat bit him on the nose. It's also where Leland Gaunt set up his shop Needful Things on Main Street, then watched from the sidelines as he pitted neighbor against neighbor, in the name of greed. Pop Verrill had a store there too; he fixed all sorts of things at the Emporium Galorium, but after tinkering with Kevin Delevan's haunted Polaroid Sun Camera, he knew he had to have it, and he paid dearly for it.

Opposite: You *can* get there from here—a bridge connecting New Hampshire and Maine.
Above: A sign welcomes travelers to the Pine Tree State, otherwise known as Stephen King's Maine Haunt.

Speaking of southern Maine, what about that strange mist that rolled into Bridgton? Folks blame the Arrowhead Project—the government's always up to something, wouldn't you say?—and while you're at it, give the eastern seaboard a wide berth if you have any business at small airports. There's a Cessna that touches down and leaves death in its wake—a fly-by-night vampire lives in the cargo hold of the plane by day, then harvests fresh blood at remote county airports where there's liable to be few, if any, witnesses, and certainly no survivors after he does his hellish work.

No doubt about it, there are a lot of places not on the map that remain uncharted territory—Stephen King country, where extraordinary things can happen to ordinary people.

This book—unlike all the other books about King—is principally a visual tour of Stephen King's Maine, buttressed by text to tell you the story behind the pictures.

As King points out in *Bare Bones* (1988), Maine's geographic distance from other states discourages the casual traveler. And if the distance doesn't intimidate, there are the forbidding winters. Termed "the kingdom of the cold" by Charles C. Calhoun in the guidebook *Maine* (1994), it's the Frigidaire state. Though accessible by air—Portland and Bangor have airports large enough to handle jets—and by car (I-95 parallels U.S. Route 1), Maine is still a good jaunt from anywhere in the United States, which is one reason why King decided to settle in the Pine Tree state.

If you are an armchair traveler, this book is your passport to King's home state. Beginning with an overview of his career, this book will take you on a tour of his life in Maine, tell you about Stephen and Tabitha King's philanthropy, take you to some of King's most famous fictional haunts in Maine and out west, and give you the lowdown on King and moviemaking in Maine. The resource listings that follow provide information on King and detailed information on travel resources for the destinations in *Stephen King Country*.

Obviously, considering King's prolificacy, the text of the book could be considerably longer, detailing every novel and short story, but that's beyond the scope of this book. My goal is to show you enough to whet your appetite and then let you go off on your own adventure.

ACKNOWLEDGMENTS

Jan Strnad—an old friend who left the exciting world of Wichita, Kansas, behind to move to Los Angeles (go figure)—has a web page on which he posts a weekly diary. There he defines a writer as "a guy who sits in a small room and types for a living."

So true! It's a dog's life, another writer once said, but it's the only life worth living. True for me, true for Jan, and certainly true for the indefatigable Stephen J. Spignesi, another writer friend who goads me into trying to keep up with his prolific output. Here, then, in no specific order, are the good angels that lent a hand when I needed it or provided the indispensable moral support, for a book that was a real pleasure to write and photograph:

Stuart Bernstein, my literary agent, who tirelessly campaigned on my behalf and found this book the perfect home, Running Press. Caroline Tiger, my editor at Running Press, whose enthusiasm for this book buoyed my spirits considerably, and whose editorial acumen measurably improved the manuscript. Thanks for making me look good. Also at Running Press: Bryn Ashburn, who designed the book with elegance and style. Stephen J. Spignesi, indisputably the King of Pop Trivia, who has published four books about King, all of which I commend to your attention. David Lowell and Kevin Quigley, two gentlemen who took time out of their schedules to drive around Maine with me—on a week that was one long, rainy season—to assist in the photography. Charles Campo and Jill Bennett of the *Bangor Daily News*, who provided (once again) photos on a moment's notice. Folks, it's always a pleasure to stop by the office, drink all your coffee, eat all your donuts, burn out your photocopying machines, and commandeer your microfilm machine. (Hey, just kidding!) Penney and Stuart Tinker, and all the fine folks at Betts Bookstore. These people are the salt of the earth and I'm enormously pleased to be able to finally have the perfect Stephen King book project in which to thank them. Colleen Doran, one of my dearest friends who always is there when I need to commiserate about the freelancing life. My wife, Mary, who marvels at my cheery disposition in the last stages of finishing up a book project, when I'm under pressure that would crack an ordinary man. (In truth, if you want to hear a *real* horror story, ask any writer's wife what the writer is really like when writing a book.)

*Like all great writers of Gothic horror, King
is a storyteller of startling images and metaphors,
which linger long in the memory and would seem
to spring from a collective unconscious and
thoroughly domestic American soil. His fellow
writers admire him for his commitment to the craft
of fiction and the generosity of his involvement
in the literary community.*

—Joyce Carol Oates, introducing Stephen King at a public talk at Princeton University, April 16, 1997

In November 1997, New American Library's greatest fear became a full-blown nightmare, the kind you'd find in a Stephen King novel.

After many years of publishing his books at NAL (an imprint of Penguin USA), rumors flew that Stephen King would soon be shopping around his new novel, *Bag of Bones*. Though NAL put on its best face, the smart money was on King's departure, the only question being which publisher would soon enjoy the cachet—financial and otherwise—of having Stephen King among its stable of authors.

Predictably, *Bag of Bones* prompted every publisher who saw it to draw up a meaty proposal. They knew it would command a high price tag, commensurate with King's

Bag of Bones, King's first novel with Scribner (published September 1998) after almost twenty years of publishing with Viking and New American Library.

estimated value in the marketplace: $17 million per book. King, who sells more than a million in hardcover and up to three million in paperback of each new novel, is a steady producer, with a guaranteed best-seller (or two) every year.

When the dust settled and the smoke cleared, King had jumped ship, leaving NAL behind.

Opting for a profit-sharing plan, King packed up his literary bags and moved uptown to Simon & Schuster, to its Scribner imprint, a move that set off seismic shock waves as other authors began thinking how to improve their lot. (Another Simon & Schuster author, Clive Cussler, was the first to deep-six his standard royalty arrangement for a profit-sharing plan. Others will surely follow.)

At stake for Scribner: millions of dollars and the daunting marketing challenge of broadening King's audience by selling him to the mainstream à la Tom Clancy or John Grisham, instead of falling back on the tried-and-true game plan of marketing him as the "Master of Pop Dread," the "Demon Fabulist," the "indisputable King of Horror," or "the most successful horror writer in history"—as *Time* termed him in its cover story, "King of Horror" (October 6, 1986).

King is understandably weary of posing as "America's best-loved boogeyman" (his self-characterization), which was a convenient marketing handle in the beginning of his career but, over the long haul, has proven limiting.

THE EARLY YEARS

Stephen King's story began on September 21, 1947, when he was born at the General Hospital in Portland, Maine. The only natural-born son of Donald and Ruth King, two-year-old Stephen saw his family suddenly shrink in size when his father—whose name was Donald Spansky before he legally changed it to King—took a walk, literally, abandoning his family. Saying he was going out for a pack of cigarettes, Donald King left behind his wife, young Stephen, and adopted son, David, and was never heard from again.

Scrambling to make ends meet, Ruth King kept what was left of her family together by living with relatives in Fort Wayne, Indiana, and Stratford, Connecticut. Eventually settling down in Durham, Maine, she shouldered the additional responsibility of caring for her ailing parents, then in their eighties.

At a time when other kids begin to seriously explore the world at large, Stephen King—an ungainly youth, oversized for his age, and clearly a social outsider, a misfit—explored a world within, dreaming up stories that took him as far away as possible from Durham, Maine, a rural town off the beaten track.

The King home was near what locals called Methodist's Corner,

Above: Maine General Hospital in Portland, where Stephen King was born on September 21, 1947.
Below: The West Durham United Methodist Church, where the Kings attended services, is near King's childhood home in Durham.

An office-model Underwood typewriter, similar to the one that was King's constant companion while growing up.

so named because of the West Durham United Methodist Church, which stands at a nearby intersection. From the front porch of their modest two-story house, Stephen King could see across an empty, windswept field to Aunt Evelyn and Uncle Oren's house.

Stephen King remembers how difficult life was in those days. In an interview with *WB*, Waldenbooks's free magazine, he said he had grown up poor, and that when the well went dry in the summer, there was no more water in the house. The blue outhouse in the back was where, he told another interviewer, he sat and contemplated his life; and in the winter, he and his brother were literally steaming when they returned from hot showers at their aunt and uncle's home.

Though King had friends locally—Donald Flaws, Brian and Douglas Hall, and principally Chris Chesley, who collaborated with King on self-published books —he often preferred his solitude, so he could write. His constant companion was a battered Underwood typewriter that belonged to his older brother, David, who used it for typing on the waxy mimeograph stencils for *Dave's Rag*, a self-published neighborhood newspaper.

In 1962, Stephen King commuted to high school in nearby Lisbon Falls, Maine, a mill town to the northeast. Along with the other kids from Durham, he rode in a converted hearse that belonged to Mike's Taxi Service of Lisbon.

A clean-cut King in the Lisbon High School yearbook, circa 1966. (Photo courtesy of the *Bangor Daily News*)

Clearly not in the elevated ranks of the caste system that characterized high school society—the upper echelon occupied by the jocks and student council members—Stephen King was a large youth, a nearsighted "four-eyes" with thick lenses.

Because he was not a jock who would cover himself with glory on the gridiron—in fact, he got cleat marks up his back as a left tackle on the football team—and not an egghead, King had to find his own identity, his own niche, and so defined himself in terms of his writing, which drew some unwanted attention. After self-publishing *The Village Vomit*, a parody of the school newspaper, King found himself with the choice of facing a suspension or—making the punishment fit the crime—serving a stint as a writer for the local newspaper, the *Lisbon Enterprise*.

Under the watchful eye of its editor, John Gould, Stephen King learned everything he needed to know about writing successfully—in ten minutes. (Earning while he learned, he got a penny for every two words for his sports journalism.) Writing was, King realized, an agreeable way to make a buck. It was also his one-way ticket out of rural Maine, but his breakthrough was still years away.

From 1966 to 1970, Stephen King—following in his adopted brother's footsteps—

moved to Orono, where he attended the University of Maine. As UMO professor Burton Hatlen pointed out, UM was where bright Mainers went if they couldn't afford a prestigious Ivy League school.

Attending college during America's most turbulent time in recent memory—when the fight for civil rights and for women's rights was raging against the backdrop of the Vietnam War—Stephen King was determined to make the most of his education and broaden his worldview.

A passionate idealist, King was active in student politics, and took a vehement stand against U.S. involvement in Vietnam. King was an advocate of popular literature, despite its unpopularity among his peers and professors in the English department; an outspoken columnist for the college newspaper, *The Maine Campus* (his column was titled "King's Garbage Truck"); and a vociferous public speaker and actor in student productions. Stephen King soaked up everything the college environment had to offer.

Stephen King and friend perform at a high school concert in 1966. (Lisbon High School Yearbook)

A determined writer, King frequently published fiction and poetry in college literary magazines and, with the encouragement of four professors in particular—Jim Bishop, Edward "Ted" Holmes, Burton Hatlen, and Carroll E. Terrell—continued to write his distinctive brand of compulsively readable fiction.

While an undergraduate, Stephen King began writing book-length fiction: *Getting It On* (a study of terror, about a boy who holds his classmates hostage), *The Long Walk* (a science-fiction novel, set in the near future, about the Walkers who voluntarily endure a death march until only one remains alive—the winner can get anything he wishes), and *Sword in the Darkness* (a naturalist novel set in Harding, Maine).

Though none of the novels sold, King's short fiction fared better. King sold two short stories, "The Glass Floor" in 1967 followed by "The Reaper's Image" in 1969, for thirty-five dollars each to *Startling Mystery Stories*, a digest-sized pulp magazine.

During his senior year, while working part-time at the university library, Stephen King met Tabitha Jane Spruce, a kindred spirit who shared his enthusiasm for writing. Theirs was not, as Douglas Winter points out in his biography, *Stephen King: The Art of Darkness*, an auspicious beginning:

> One day, she was crossing the campus to the library with a friend. "He pointed ahead of us to this enormous, shambling person in cut-off gum rubbers. Talk about hippie—this was serious hippiedom in front of me."
>
> My friend said, "Do you know who that is? That's Steve King, and he is going to be working with you this summer." And I said, sarcastically, "I think I'm in love."
>
> When they eventually met in the library stacks, it was not exactly

King speaks out at a protest rally at the University of Maine at Orono, which he attended from 1966 to 1970. (University of Maine at Orono yearbook)

love at first sight. "I was a lot more impressed with him than he was with me," she recalls.

Tabitha Jane Spruce discovered that you can't judge a book by its cover, so to speak. Her initial impressions of him as "serious hippiedom" soon gave way to a deep respect for his seriousness as a writer. "All he cared about," she told Winter in *Stephen King: The Art of Darkness*, "was getting everything he could out of school and writing his head off." A serious poet herself, Tabitha Spruce understood the kind of commitment it took for him to persevere as a writer with professional aspirations.

Stephen King graduated from UMO on June 5, 1970. In what he termed his "birth announcement," published in the May 21, 1970, issue of *The Maine Campus*, a world-weary Stephen King wrote in "King's Garbage Truck:" "This boy has shown evidences of some talent, although at this point it is impossible to tell if he is just a flash in the pan or if he has real possibilities. It seems obvious that he has learned a great deal at the University of Maine at Orono."

King moved into a cabin near the Stillwater River and, despite his inability to sell a novel, began writing *The Dark Tower*. After hammering out the first few chapters on his manual Underwood typewriter, he showed the sheaf of pages to Chris Chesley, whom he knew would tell him exactly what he thought of the work. Chesley read the first few pages and told King that it was the best thing he had written in years. But for now, more pressing matters were at hand; namely, King had to find full-time employment, since writing wasn't going to pay the bills.

The conventional wisdom—then and now—is that a college degree is a ticket to success, a guarantee that the recipient won't find himself in a dead-end job or, in the vernacular of teenagers today, a McJob. Unable to find a teaching job, King took a McJob, pumping gas for $1.25 an hour at a gas station near Orono. He graduated from that to working at an industrial laundry in Bangor, where he earned $1.60 an hour.

Chris Chesley, King's childhood friend, at the Harmony Grove Cemetery.

The stint at the laundry, however, was not entirely a waste of time; in addition to paying the bills, King eventually transmuted the experience into fiction.

THE SEVENTIES: PUBLISH OR PERISH

In January 1971, Stephen and Tabitha married. Wearing a borrowed suit, Stephen King had to take time off from his job at the laundry. Although the management wished him well, he was still docked a half day's pay.

Like most young newlyweds, the Kings had a difficult time financially. In fact, money was impossibly tight. Working full-time at the laundry, Stephen King was the sole breadwinner; Tabitha King, then a junior in college, was still working toward her history degree. The birth of their first child, Naomi, added to the financial stress.

By this time King was selling short fiction to *Cavalier* magazine, but because he was paid only on publication, cash flow was a problem. Realizing that he'd need to sell book-length fiction to obtain a respectable advance, he decided to submit *Getting It On* to Doubleday. King sent his manuscript to the attention of the editor of *The Parallax View*, who had since left the house, asking that his projects—including *The Parallax View*—be handled by Bill Thompson. (Years later, Thompson would discover another author, a lawyer-turned-writer by the name of John Grisham.)

The drop-off point in downtown Bangor for the New Franklin Laundry, where King earned sixty dollars a week working full-time.

Tabitha King and tabby at home in Bangor. (Photo courtesy of the *Bangor Daily News*)

In contrast to earlier rebuffs—*The Long Walk* failed to win a Bennett Cerf-sponsored first novel competition, and *Sword in the Darkness* was rejected by a dozen publishers, including Doubleday—*Getting It On* received a tentative show of interest. It was about time, thought King, who was still working at the New Franklin Laundry. (Tabitha also worked in Bangor, as a waitress at the Dunkin' Donuts on Main Street.)

Fortunately, Thompson was enthusiastic about *Getting It On*, which he felt showed a lot of promise. Unfortunately, Thompson's enthusiasm wasn't shared by the decision makers at Doubleday, and King's high hopes were dashed.

King later wrote, in an essay collected in *Fear Itself*, that "Doubleday declined, a painful blow for me, because I had been allowed to entertain some hope for an extraordinarily long time, and had rewritten the book a third time, trying to bring it into line with what Doubleday's publishing board would accept."

Understandably crestfallen, King realized that he wasn't going to set the literary world on fire anytime soon, so when a teaching position opened at Hampden Academy—the school where he had student-taught as a UMO senior—he took the job at a starting salary of $6,400.

Those years—from 1971 to 1973—were the most difficult years of King's life. Always short of money and unable to sell anything but short stories, King justifiably questioned his future as a writer. During his 1972 Christmas vacation from school, King cranked out *The Running Man*, his fourth novel, which he hoped would sell quickly and alleviate some of the financial pressure the Kings were experiencing. Like the other novels, this one, submitted to Doubleday, was in due course rejected.

Living in a rented double-wide trailer in Hermon, Maine, a small town west of Bangor on Route 2, the Kings added Joseph to their family in June 1972, and the financial situation—already critical—stretched to the breaking point. The pressures of being a young father, without the benefit of having had his own father as a role model, and of being under constant financial pressure, finally took its toll on King.

In early winter of 1972, King suffered from writer's block, the inevitable result of his stressful life. Incapable of writing a new story, King picked up the bare bones of one he had begun earlier that summer, which he hoped would be a quick sale to *Cavalier*.

It was a story about an ugly duckling of a girl named Carietta White, who was constantly being dumped on by her classmates. But after writing a few pages, King threw them in the trash, realizing that he was writing on a subject he knew nothing about: a girl having her first menstrual period in a girl's locker room at school.

Hampden Academy, where King taught from 1971 to 1973. During this time his third and fourth novels were rejected by publishers.

Tabitha fished the pages out and encouraged Stephen to continue. He persisted, more out of dogged determination than anything else. Unlike a novel, which required a lot of time and might not sell, a short story had a high probability of selling, so he completed the story and, to his horror, realized it had grown in length—it was so long that he could forget selling it to Nye Willden, his editor at *Cavalier*.

Instead of a short story, King had on his hands a literary oddity: definitely too long for *Cavalier*, or any other magazine for that matter, but too short to be a novel.

In an essay published years later in *Fear Itself*, King wrote, "When I finished, I had a novella that was ninety-eight single-spaced manuscript pages long. I think it would be fair to say that I detested it. . . . The length was wrong and the ending was terribly downbeat."

King decided to go for broke. In for a penny, in for a pound, he invested even more time in the story, fleshing it out with bogus documentation—imaginary quotes from real-world publications, like *Esquire*—to beef up the wordage to short-novel length. Even then, King was reluctant to send it out. He had written what he "considered to be a certified loser."

At the prompting of Bill Thompson, who was fishing for another manuscript, King reluctantly sent in *Carrie* and got the usual nibble, but nothing more, which by now he learned was no cause for premature celebration.

King relaxes with a *Mad Magazine* in the teacher's lounge at Hampden Academy. (Hampden Academy Yearbook)

This time, King's expectations were considerably muted. He had learned the hard way that just because an editor *likes* the book doesn't mean it's going to sell. At Doubleday it also had to pass muster at the acquisitions meeting, attended not only by editors but also by marketing, sales, and management people.

King crossed his fingers and again, under specific editorial guidance from Thompson, King rewrote the book in the hope that it would increase the odds in his favor. At Thompson's invitation, King met the editor for lunch in New York. It was February 1973, and King was the country mouse visiting the city mouse. Strapped for money, King borrowed the bus fare from his grandparents.

In "On Becoming a Brand Name," an essay published in *Fear Itself*, King recounts his first trip to New York, which turned out to be a comedy of errors—he arrived too early, wore brand-new shoes that gave him blisters, ate fettuccini that speckled his beard, and committed other social faux pas, but Thompson and another Doubleday staffer took it in stride. Their real purpose was to size each other up, to see what kind of chemistry existed between the writer and his potential editor, since there was the likelihood that *Carrie* was going to sell.

Recalling that previous submissions from King were eventually rejected by Doubleday, Thompson was guardedly optimistic about the odds that Doubleday would buy *Carrie*, though privately he felt the book would survive the acquisitions gauntlet. On that note, King headed back home, buoyed by the thought that maybe this time his luck would change.

Leaving the glamorous world of publishing behind, King boarded a Greyhound at the Port Authority for his return trip to Hermon. Now, all he could do was wait to hear from Thompson, but not by phone, which the Kings had removed to save money. (In an emergency, they used a neighbor's phone.)

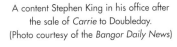

A month later, King got the word. The telegram, sent to King's house, was short and sweet: "CARRIE" OFFICIALLY A DOUBLEDAY BOOK. $2,500 ADVANCE AGAINST ROYALTIES. CONGRATS, KID—THE FUTURE LIES AHEAD. BILL.

Tabitha King went next door to call Stephen at school. Late that afternoon, when King got home, Chris Chesley—who was attending UMO and rooming with the Kings—"got out of the way," as he recalled, to let the Kings enjoy their cathartic moment.

After fourteen years of pounding the typewriter and collecting enough rejection slips to paper his wall, Stephen King finally sold a novel.

A content Stephen King in his office after the sale of *Carrie* to Doubleday. (Photo courtesy of the *Bangor Daily News*)

King knew that he couldn't afford to quit his day job—not yet, anyway—and continued to write in the evenings while he awaited the publication of *Carrie*. King also realized that, insofar as *Carrie* was concerned, the publishing odds were stacked against him. He lacked a brand name; Doubleday couldn't justify a big budget for advertising a first book; personal appearances at bookstores would be exercises in futility, since customers don't show up to get books signed by unknowns; and the best that could be hoped for in terms of media coverage was a write-up in the local paper, the *Bangor Daily News*. (The first profile on King as a teacher-turned-writer did appear in that paper. It was written by David Bright, who was King's editor at *The Maine Campus* during the "King's Garbage Truck" days.)

Carrie, in short, would have to find its own way into the world. The question: Would the booksellers stand by the book? A $5.95 hardcover, the book had only one thing going for it—a helluva story—but would that be enough? For the moment, however, the $2,500 seemed heaven-sent. The Kings could now afford to reconnect the phone, though they soon had another problem: their landlord evicted them—for

reasons unknown—from their rented double-wide, and the Kings moved to the blue-collar part of town in nearby Bangor, to Sanford Street, where they rented a second-floor walk-up apartment.

On Mother's Day in 1973, Stephen King got the phone call that forever changed his life. Thompson called with news about a subsidiary sale for *Carrie*. New American Library, then an imprint of Penguin USA, had made a preemptive early bid, concerned that if the book went to auction, it'd go for even more. For rights to publish the paperback, NAL was offering a staggering $400,000, of which King would get half.

For days afterward, King was worried sick that he had misheard the amount, that it was not the grand sum he thought he had heard, but instead $40,000. Half of that, he reasoned, was still enough to allow him to quit teaching and write full-time, though on a modest budget.

King had heard right, though, and the windfall meant that he could now afford to quit teaching, if he wanted to. But after two years of teaching, King found it hard to leave. A teacher well-liked by his students and well-respected by his peers, he'd have to give up the social interaction that he enjoyed and face the solitude of the blank page on a daily basis. In addition, his students were now asking his advice on writing and on how to get published, and he wanted to help the more promising writers.

It seems fair to say that King knew he'd eventually make a decision in favor of writing full-time, which is what he felt was his mission in life, but it didn't make the

Sanford Street in Bangor, where the Kings moved after being evicted from their double-wide trailer in Hermon.

decision any easier. He chose to leave his job, but as circumstances would prove, he would not put teaching behind him forever.

Carrie was published in 1974, followed by 'Salem's Lot (1975), The Shining (1977), Rage (formerly titled Getting It On, published in 1977 under King's pen name, Richard Bachman), The Stand (1978), and Night Shift (1978).

Clearly, King, a brand name in the making, would forever be associated with supernatural fiction, but at the time that didn't concern him. (Years later, when he began writing regional and mainstream fiction, the supernatural label came back to haunt him, scaring away potential customers.)

In terms of his book contracts, what seemed like a good idea at the time turned out to be a bad one. Instead of taking money earned when due in the form of book royalties, King had signed a contract that pooled his earnings and gave him an "allowance," so to speak, which guaranteed steady income for the years to come. However, based on his allowance of $50,000 a year, it would take sixty years for Doubleday to pay him what they already owed him. In other words, he might never live to see a full payout. But the contract was iron-clad and, adding financial insult to financial injury, King's advances remained low, despite the guarantee of paperback sales to NAL.

Even more galling, a pernicious clause required him to share half of all reprint sales

 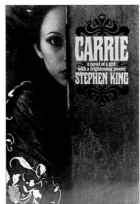

Left: Note the absence of a byline on this paperback edition of Carrie—because King was an unknown in 1974, putting his name on the cover would not have helped sales.
Right: Carrie in hardcover (Doubleday). As King is fond of saying in interviews, he made Carrie and Carrie made him.

with the publisher. On the face of it, it seemed fair, but to King's mind, this was simply a commissionable sale worth the standard agent's fee of ten percent.

Doubleday said the fifty percent split—an industry standard—was non-negotiable, which proved to be the final straw for King, already aggravated by Doubleday's refusal to issue a limited edition of The Stand.

Bill Thompson's perception mirrored King's own that the firm's best-selling author was being taken for granted. It was, King realized, time to move to another publishing house where the contracts would be more favorable and the executives might remember who he was when he visited the office. (Thompson lamented that each time King came to the office, he had to be reintroduced to the key executives.)

In the winter of 1976, at a literary party in New York, King met an agent who represented writers in the fantasy genre. Kirby McCauley, a transplanted Midwesterner, had read only one book by King at the time of the party—'Salem's Lot—but after meeting King, and recalling how impressed he was with that book, he wanted to add the author to his growing list of clients.

McCauley later recalled in an interview in the fanzine *Castle Rock*, "I partly saw his success growing. I saw that he was going to get bigger and bigger. But . . . I can't say I foresaw Steve King being the literary phenomenon of the last half of the twentieth century." Like McCauley, Doubleday clearly didn't see King as a defining superstar, either, and adamantly refused to budge on the fifty percent division of money on reprint sales.

Left: *The Shining* (Doubleday) was King's first hardcover best-seller.
Right: *Night Shift* (Doubleday) was King's first published collection of short fiction.

It proved to be the final straw for King, who realized that his divorce from Doubleday was imminent, but he knew he didn't want to act again as his agent and have, as he put it, a fool for a client. He needed professional representation, and quickly. Enter Kirby McCauley, who broke King into the slicks, then engineered his move to New American Library with a three-book, $2.5-million deal.

The deal put King, and McCauley as well, into a new league. For King, it meant that he could concentrate on writing books and leave the turgidly written contracts and subsequent negotiations to his agent.

In retrospect, to be fair to Doubleday, the firm did launch King's career; and although their hardcovers were published in cheap-jacket editions with glue bindings that were guaranteed to fall apart under repeated readings, Doubleday did sell *Carrie* to Hollywood, goosing King's popularity as a pop culture writer. They also ensured that all of his books were sold in inexpensive mass market paperbacks; and Doubleday built King's core audience until his sales reached critical mass, helping *The Shining* to become his first hardcover best-seller.

Even with all that, you have to wonder about the lack of imagination shown by top management, whose inflexibility cost them millions in lost income. Best-selling authors are, after all, rare beasts, and sometimes they need a little extra attention.

From 1974 to 1978, the Kings moved frequently. After the paperback sale of *Carrie*, they moved to a rented house in North Windham. Wanting a change of scenery from Maine, King temporarily moved his family to Boulder, Colorado, in 1974, returning the following year to Bridgton, Maine.

In 1977 King moved the family to England. A planned one-year stay was cut short to three months. Returning to Maine, he sold the Bridgton home and bought a contemporary home on Kezar Lake in Center Lovell—the Kings' summer house, which they still own today.

In 1978 the Kings moved temporarily to Orrington, Maine, where they rented a two-story house within a stone's throw of Route 15.

King's home office, circa 1988. (Photo courtesy of the *Bangor Daily News*)

THE EIGHTIES: THE KING OF HORROR

In 1979 Viking published *The Dead Zone* in hardcover. A striking departure in design from King's Doubleday books, this book looked sharp: its cover design recalled the imaginative designs used by NAL, which recognized the fact that book covers should be designed like mini-posters.

Unlike *The Dead Zone*, *The Long Walk*—written under the pseudonym of Richard Bachman and published in 1979 by New American Library—was issued in stealth mode, going out undetected. Like the first Bachman book, *Rage*, *The Long Walk* was perceived by the book trade as genre fiction, as an inexpensive paperback novel by a relatively unknown writer, and it was all but ignored.

In 1980 the Kings finally settled in Maine for the long haul; they bought a winter home in Bangor, which would in time become their home base. That year, Stanley Kubrick's controversial film version of *The Shining* was released to generally positive reviews, buttressed by King's initially positive comments. King, though, cared little for the film and later voiced his opinions loudly, which would come back to haunt him years later.

In the eighties, King lived up to his reputation as a prolific author, publishing with a regularity that satisfied his publishers, the bookstores, and his millions of fans. In 1980 he published *Firestarter*; in 1981, *Danse Macabre*, *Cujo*, and *Roadwork* (a Bachman book); in 1982, *The Dark Tower: The Gunslinger* (at a small press called Donald M. Grant, Publisher), *Different Seasons* (a collection of novellas, only one of which was supernatural in nature), *Creepshow* (a comic book), and *The Running Man* (a Bachman book); in 1983, *Christine*, *Pet Sematary*, *Cycle of the Werewolf* (later reprinted as *Silver Bullet* for the movie tie-in edition); in 1984, *The Talisman*, *The Eyes of the Dragon* (from Philtrum Press), and *Thinner* (the Bachman book that blew his cover); in 1985, *Skeleton Crew* and *The Bachman Books*; in 1986, *Silver Bullet* and *IT*; in 1987, *The Dark Tower II: The Drawing of the Three*, the trade edition of *The Eyes of the Dragon*, *The Tommyknockers*, and the masterful psychological suspense novel, *Misery*; in 1988, no King novel, owing to King's non-book commitments; and in 1989, King closed out the decade with "My Pretty Pony" (a short story published as a sumptuous limited edition book) and *The Dark Half*.

It was a time of literary experimentation for King, who realized that his readers' voracious appetites, true to the sentiments of the decade, could not be sated; the more he published, the more they wanted, like the carnivorous plant in *The Little Shop of Horrors* that pleads "Feed me!" Fortunately King's publisher was glad to oblige.

Unlike King's fiction, in which his plain Maine voice is a constant, his film adaptations were all over the map in terms of quality and fidelity to his stories. Too much, it seemed, depended on the vision of the director and his ability to translate King's fictional voice to film. There were some notable exceptions: *Carrie* (1976), a Brian De Palma film; *The Dead Zone* (1983), a David Cronenberg film; and *Stand By Me* (1986), Rob Reiner's film that exposed King to a mainstream audience who were surprised to learn that it was based on a King short story, "The Body."

But mainstream filmgoers had inextricably linked King with horror, which was not surprising after a string of average, or below-average, films that appeared in quick succession—one critic termed one summer's offerings "the Stephen King Film of the Month Club."

Nothing exceeds like excess, and the quick succession of *Christine* (1983), *Children of the Corn* (1984), *Firestarter* (1984), *Cat's Eye* (1985), *Silver Bullet* (1985), and King's own *Maximum Overdrive* (1986) (which he wrote and directed) tarnished the once shiny luster of King's name in the film community.

Hollywood, in effect, had killed the goose that laid the golden eggs by flooding the market, eager to capitalize on King's good name, which obviously worked wonders in bookstores worldwide. But as King fans knew, whatever it was that they found in his books, they seldom found in his movies. King's distinctive voice, they complained, was lost in the translation, an assessment with which King reluctantly agreed. (In retrospect, it seems obvious that King's supernatural stories suffered most in the translation; King's mainstream stories like "The Body," which inspired *Stand By Me*, and *Misery*, more easily survived the process virtually unchanged.)

In Bangor, on the home front, the Kings had become pillars of the community through their increasing involvement with charities, fundraising activities, and business ownership of a local radio station.

An authorized newsletter about King—a notable exception to his "no merchandising" rule—began publication in 1985. It is based in Bangor and was originally edited and published by King's sister-in-law and full-time secretary, Stephanie Leonard. (Leonard's brother Chris later took over, simultaneously continuing his job as the general manager of WZON.)

King had put his unmistakable mark on the eighties. He proved, as an author, that his name had currency. As one reader pointed out in a letter to Stephen King, "All I have to see is the name 'Stephen King' and I know it's going to be a good book."

Thought not all of King's critics would agree with that assessment, his fans sure did, and they didn't give a damn what the snooty book critics said about his books, which, as A. J. Budrys pointed out in *Fantasy & Science Fiction* magazine, were "review-proof."

King's fans, in short, were legion.

THE NINETIES: UPPING THE ANTE

To my mind, King's early books—the ones at Doubleday—show the work of a demon-driven writer whose fiction has a distinctive visceral feel that cuts to the bone. These were the days when King clearly wrote for himself, largely unaffected by his growing readership and by the critics.

In the middle period—the eighties—King's prolificacy and desire to experiment with his prose inevitably resulted in a wide range of material, with varying results: on one hand, there was the bloated and diffuse science fiction/horror novel, *The Tommyknockers*; on the other, a sharply focused study of psychological terror, *Misery*.

Unlike the eighties, the nineties would be for King a decade of closure, both professionally and personally. On the book front, the decade started off with the publication of *Four Past Midnight*, a novella collection that, though clearly not another *Different Seasons* in mainstream appeal, was nonetheless an impressive collection, and seemed like the work of a more mature writer stretching himself. (One of the stories, "The Sun Dog," set in Castle Rock, would be a narrative bridge to the last Castle Rock story, *Needful Things*.)

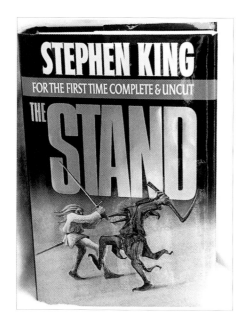

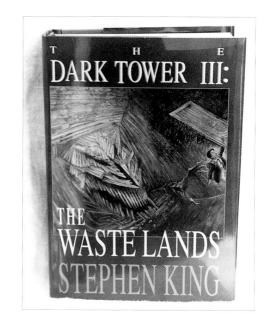

Evidence of King's growth could also be seen in his other book offering that year: *The Stand*, republished in a greatly revised and expanded edition. Long awaited by King's fans who argued about virtually everything regarding things King, *The Stand*, all agreed, was their favorite novel.

In addition to publishing a textually preferred trade edition of *The Stand*, King finally saw it published in an elegant, limited edition, which was all the more sweet because the publisher was Doubleday. (Years earlier, Doubleday had forced King to cut the book and refused to issue a limited edition, citing book club competition.)

In stark contrast to the low-quality trade editions Doubleday published of King's early books, the house did a magnificent job on the limited edition of *The Stand*, due in great part to the vision of Peter Schneider, who was well acquainted with how a limited edition ought to look. (Schneider ran his own small press, Hill House Publishers, which issued, among other titles, Peter Straub's *Ghost Story*.)

In 1991 King explored Castle Rock one last time in a long novel, *Needful Things*. Deciding that it was time to move on, to explore other fictional themes and worlds, King laid waste to the town in a spectacular fire. Castle Rock, like Jerusalem's Lot in *'Salem's Lot*, was history, he said.

That year King also published the latest volume of his Dark Tower series, *The Dark Tower III: The Wastelands*. He followed with two novels connected by remembrances of things past: *Gerald's Game* (1992) and *Dolores Claiborne* (1993).

In *Gerald's Game*, a bondage game gone awry triggers Jessie Burlingame's long-repressed memories of child abuse (a theme King explored earlier in "The Library Policeman," in *Four Past Midnight*). In its companion book, titled after the main

Left: This "complete and uncut edition" (as the publisher termed it) in hardcover of *The Stand* (1990), is significant for King who opposed Doubleday's abridgment of its original 1978 edition.
Right: *Dark Tower III: The Wastelands* (1991), like the other books in this series, was published in hardcover by Donald M. Grant and reprinted by NAL.

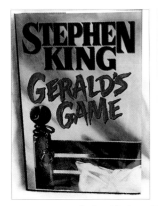

Left: *Gerald's Game* (1992) explores female empowerment—a theme King first touched on in *Carrie*.
Right: *Rose Madder* (1995) explores the domestic horror of spousal abuse, as Rose Daniels escapes from policeman Norman Daniels, her monstrous husband who is intent on tracking her down.

character, Dolores Claiborne must convince the police that she has nothing to do with Vera Donovan's death, despite the suspicious circumstances.

In 1993, King issued his third collection of short fiction, *Nightmares & Dreamscapes*, his most diverse collection, which included poetry, a long non-fiction piece on Little League baseball, and short stories from diverse sources, dating back to the early years when college publications were his only publishing option.

In 1994, King published *Insomnia*, a complex novel in which the threads from several of his other books—notably the Dark Tower books—come together. Told in a slow, measured pace, the tempo picks up as the book reaches its climax, set at the Derry Civic Center (modeled after the Bangor Auditorium and Civic Center). *Rose Madder*, published in 1995, was followed by his self-published *Six Stories*.

Around this time changes were in the air, and King would inevitably be affected. Merger mania and consolidation had become the buzzwords in the book trade in the late nineties, and two lions—NAL and G.P. Putnam—joined forces.

The atmosphere, King decided, had suddenly become frigid. King found his king-of-the-hill position usurped by Tom Clancy, whose book contracts dwarf King's book deals. (Clancy, who tapped into a large mainstream audience, enjoyed sales that averaged a million more copies in hardcover than any King novel.) Understandably frustrated at being actively marketed as *only* a spook writer, King, too, wanted to tap into the mainstream audience—the same one that knows his work not through his books but through television, film, and mainstream magazines like *The New Yorker*.

Nineteen ninety-six proved to be a banner year for King, who had a record eight books on the best-seller lists: six installments of a serialized novel, *The Green Mile*, paving the way for "twinner" books, *Desperation* (by King) and *The Regulators* (by Bachman), which featured the same characters in different settings.

All, however, was not well in Stephen's kingdom. Concerned that his constant readers were being overcharged for the individual installments of *The Green Mile*, King voiced his concerns. The publisher responded, saying that because of markdowns needed by the chain stores to compete with Internet-based booksellers and warehouse clubs that discounted up to forty percent, each installment would have to be priced to compensate—a curious notion, since the original idea was to publish inexpensive paperbacks.

And yet another cause of grave concern for King: he found himself debating the merits of issuing the "twinner novels" (*Desperation* and *The Regulators*) under their respective authors' names. NAL wanted to increase sales by issuing Bachman's *The Regulators* with cover copy that indicated it was in fact a Stephen King novel—a sore point with King, who felt that it would have defeated the purpose of publishing under a pseudonym.

NAL knew that, no matter how they advertised both books, some people would never make the connection; sales of the Bachman book, they knew, would be less than the King book, unless they blatantly made the King-Bachman connection obvious.

Though *The Green Mile* was finally published in an affordable trade paperback edition in 1997, and although its sales numbers were impressive—as were the reviews for each installment of *The Green Mile*—King was still unhappy at NAL. In fact, at that point, there was probably little that NAL could have done to please King to his satisfaction.

In 1997, King published *The Dark Tower IV: Wizard and Glass*. Readers hoped this installment would take Roland closer to the fabled and elusive Dark Tower, but the book largely recounted Roland's past, setting the stage for what will follow in the fifth book, as yet unwritten. Just as Roland would see his landscape change around him, King saw his world turn depressingly unfamiliar—and to his mind, potentially hostile.

A publishing storm was on the way. It was time, King knew, for a change.

King left for a much needed and long overdue vacation to Australia—his first visit to that country—and rode a Harley across its plains. Meanwhile, at the Frankfurt book fair in Germany, the rumors began to fly. Stateside, King's agent/lawyer/business manager Arthur Greene dropped the bombshell: King was looking for a new home, and it was time for publishers to place their bets.

A "twinner" novel with *Desperation*, *The Regulators* was published under King's pen name, Richard Bachman. (Both novels share some of the same characters, though in different settings: *Desperation* is set in Desperation, Nevada, and *The Regulators* is set in Wentworth, Ohio.)

Caught off-guard, publishers in New York scrambled to put together their offers, including—at Greene's behest—game plans on how best to market King, who was obviously unhappy with the fact that his book sales had leveled off. King, Greene knew, was looking for a publisher who would take his sales to a new level, and do so with enthusiasm, which he felt only a new publisher could do for him.

When the dust settled, Scribner—a literary imprint best known for publishing Ernest Hemingway and F. Scott Fitzgerald—emerged victorious. To paraphrase a promotional postcard NAL sent out for *Needful Things*: Stephen King bids farewell to NAL. . . . Parting is such sweet horror (for the publisher).

During all of this, NAL had put on its best face, asserting that it was still in the running, still negotiating, but it clearly didn't look like that to the book publishing community. In fact, at that point there was already speculation about whether or not NAL would wind up with the consolation prize—the paperback reprint rights—but King's new allegiance to Scribner took precedence; Pocket Books retained reprint rights.

The only other long-standing matters at NAL: the existing contracts and whether they would be renewed. (King had leased his books to NAL; he is free to take them anywhere after the leases expire in the next few years. The smart money is on his reclaiming his books and giving his lucrative backlist to Scribner and Pocket Books.)

Apparently, the goodwill that had been generated by the years of association between King and NAL's Elaine Koster—his contact at NAL since the beginning—wasn't enough to bind him to old ties. Friendship and business, King seemed to say, don't mix. A few short months later, when Elaine Koster left the firm to start her own literary agency, it was a sign of the times not only for NAL but for King as well.

In the high-stakes poker game of book publishing, King dealt NAL out and upped the ante by fundamentally changing the nature of his relationship with his new publisher. The three-book deal King signed with Scribner was as unique in its way as the NAL deal was in its time: King eschewed the standard royalty arrangement in favor of a profit-sharing plan that, in effect, made him a copublisher with a big say in how his books would be marketed, sold, and promoted.

Predictably, King's new publisher praised his imaginative deal-making, but in truth, as the book community well knew, with the world media reporting every development, what was originally supposed to be a smooth move to another house had turned chaotic, a public relations disaster for King himself. Stung by criticism in and outside the book trade, King vowed that before he went through that charade again, he'd self-publish, and he meant it.

Bag of Bones, a hefty 529-page novel, was evolutionary, his new publisher said. Characterized by King as a "haunted love story," it was clearly written to showcase a new Stephen King, one who was able to duke it out with mainstream writers like Clancy and John Grisham.

I'm willing to take that chance, King seemed to say with this book, but not when I'm hobbled with the sales-limiting title of "horrormeister." Years ago, when he was starting out, the "horror writer" label was not a concern; now, it was a grave one because it scared away potential readers, the ones who loved *The Green Mile* and raved about *Stand By Me* and *The Shawshank Redemption* in the theaters, but otherwise avoided all exposure to "Typhoid" King in the bookstore.

Bag of Bones would be the first of three books to redefine King to the book trade and to the world at large. King clearly wanted to be judged as a writer, not perceived as solely a horror writer.

As to what is in store for him long term at Scribner, it's too early to tell. But one thing is certain: Scribner is promoting and selling King's *Bag of Bones* with the kind of enthusiasm that only a new publisher can bring to bear. *Bag of Bones*, a $28 hardcover published on September 23, 1998, was simultaneously released in a $59.95 unabridged audio book read by King. Prepublication publicity included a website with audio-clips and book galleys to key reviewers and media, and book signings scheduled coast to coast.

If Scribner plays its cards right, and never gives King the impression he's being taken for granted—the perception he got at his previous publishers—the third time might prove a charm, and Scribner may remain King's publisher for the remainder of his career.

Insofar as King's fiction is concerned, if *Bag of Bones* is any indication, his best is yet to come—an exciting possibility for Scribner and for King, who can't afford to be complacent about how he's being published. (It's not the money, it's a matter of respect.)

Will King be the writer who bridges the gap between popular and critical fiction with mainstream books? It's too early to tell, but that potential exists. No matter what else, one thing is certain: King, asserts biographer Douglas Winter, best deserves the title "America's storyteller."

With all his successes, however, Stephen King has never lost sight of the reason all of these things have happened to him. In *Explorations*, the Barnes and Noble newsletter, Harlan Ellison, a writer and longtime friend of the Kings, said:

> I think the greatest enemy a serious writer has is not age or diminishing talent or the vicissitudes of the marketplace . . . I think it's your audience. They're your greatest enemy because if you write something they like, they will keep you writing it for the next fifty years. . . . I have learned my craft a lot better. I work at it very, very hard. I need to know if I can still do the work. That is all that matters to me. Success is very nice. I'm about as famous as I care to be. Yet, all I care about is the quality of the work. Can I still keep being fresh, different?

That, too, is Stephen King's most difficult challenge.

Outsiders think they are the same, these small towns—that they don't change. It's a kind of death the outsiders believe in, although they will call it "tradition" simply because it sounds more polite. It's those inside the town who know the difference —they know it but they don't see it.

—"It Grows on You," a short story by Stephen King published in *Whispers* magazine

PART 1
STEPHEN KING'S REAL MAINE HAUNTS

CHAPTER 1: MAINE BORN AND BRED

Above: Runaround Pond, home to the blood-sucking leeches immortalized in *Stand By Me*, a movie based on King's novella in *Different Seasons*, "The Body."

E ver heard of Durham, Maine? What about Lisbon Falls? North Windham? Bridgton? Center Lovell? Hermon? Orrington?

You will never find tour buses headed in the directions of these towns, taking the summer people away from the coastal towns and shopping meccas near the Interstate and U.S. Route 1 from which they rarely stray.

These are all places where Stephen King lived, places where anyone could easily lose himself for a day, a week, or even a year. These are King's Maine haunts, where he saw through his rural existence to imagine worlds that never existed. In these small towns, others saw the ordinary—places untouched by the passage of time—but he saw the extraordinary: the possibilities that could only be imagined by a young boy with an overactive imagination fueled by a desire to escape, if only to his fictional worlds, from the commonplace.

In 1958 Ruth King moved her family to this small town, which then numbered less than a thousand people. (Today, it numbers even less—the young people leave for college or for larger cities in Maine, like nearby Portland, Bangor, or Augusta, or escape out of state.)

King, then eleven years old, realized that he was stuck in Durham, at least for the time being; that his only ticket out, temporarily, was his imagination, which transformed Durham, with its rural ambience, into something far more sinister.

Even at that young age, King loved to tell stories and hammer them out on his brother's office Underwood. As his childhood friend Chris Chesley recalls:

> When I went to Stephen King's house to write stories with him, there was the sense that these things weren't just stories; when you walked inside the walls of his house, there was a sense of palpability, almost as if the characters in the stories had real weight.
>
> Imagination didn't make it real just for him—it made it real for *me*. To go inside his house was like being pulled into a different world unlike old, unimaginative Durham with its cowsheds. And that's what drew me to go see him. He had that ability. If you went inside those walls and you were at all susceptible, you would be drawn into that.
>
> And when you read stories with him, or read his writing, or participated and wrote stories with him, the stories took on weight. It was a world unto itself, and I was privileged to enter it. Even as a kid, as a teenager, King had the power to do that. It was an amazing thing.

The Kings' small, two-story house near Methodist's Corner—so named because of the church that was the community's focal point—was a mile from the Flaws' home, where his Aunt Evelyn and Uncle Oren lived. In their attic, Stephen King discovered a box of paperbacks belonging to his father, mostly horror novels, including an H. P. Lovecraft book that, wrote King, was a turning point for him. Like his father, he had a taste for weird fiction, which would not have come as a surprise to the locals, who felt that King was too introspective for his own good. In *Mr. Monster's Movie Gold*, King explains:

> My interest in horror and the fantastic wasn't looked upon with any approval whatsoever—there went young Steve King, his nose either in a lurid issue of *Tales from the Vault* or an even more lurid paperback. . . .

When he wasn't gorging himself on "poisoned" literary fruit, he haunted nearby
Runaround Pond, where he and Chris Chesley lured unsuspecting newcomers for a
swim, urging them not to swim out toward deeper waters.

What the newbies didn't realize: blood-sucking leeches stayed close to shore and
quickly attached themselves to any intruders, so when the unsuspecting youths emerged
from the water, covered with leeches, they screamed bloody horror as Chesley and King
looked on and laughed their heads off.

The leech scene would, like other memorable incidents in King's life, show up
later in his fiction; in this case, in "The Body," King's most autobiographical story,
set in Durham.

King and Chesley also slept out at the nearby cemetery, Harmony Grove, with its
mostly plain headstones that Chesley called "death's plain calling cards." (This
cemetery is prominent in 'Salem's Lot.)

Budding writers who had self-published "books" on David King's mimeograph
machine, Stephen King and Chris Chesley also haunted Durham with a movie camera

in hand. In a personal interview, Chris Chesley recalls:

Harmony Grove Cemetery, which King and his childhood friend Chris Chesley frequently haunted.

> We got hold of a movie camera. We weren't seriously trying to make a movie; we were trying to figure out how you designed a shot to make it scary. We were trying to figure out how you got the person up and down the stairs, how you got the shadows.
>
> This house on Deep Cut Road was the kind of place that had bad vibes. You didn't want to spend the night there. I don't think we ever got enough nerve to do that. It had enough feeling of previous occupancy so that you didn't want to hang around too long. It had the staircase that Steve mentions in 'Salem's Lot where Hubie Marsten hung himself.

That abandoned home on Deep Cut Road, south of Interstate 95, was the inspiration for the Marsten House, noted King years later. Like the four teenagers in "The Body," King, Chesley, and their friends had their own private hangout—the 249 Club, so named after they found a discarded sign off an apartment building. Appropriating the sign, dubbing the area in the loft behind the King house as the 249 Club, they played cards there and told tall tales.

Although most people in Durham looked around and saw only its rural plainness, King felt its seasonal rhythms, its slow pulse, and captured it all in his fiction. As Chesley points out:

> The country dirt roads, the stands of pine trees, the hayfields run to seed, the antique-copper Maine sun, all of it common, and real enough, yet within King's room, as if an actual atmosphere, as if breathed out on the air directly from the imagination of the kid who owned the typewriter, extraordinary things were vivid and real enough—more real, for an afternoon, than all the prosaic territory outside.

LISBON FALLS

Above: Lisbon Falls in the fifties.
Below: From 1962 to 1966, King commuted from Durham to attend Lisbon High School. The girl who would eventually provide the inspiration for *Carrie* was part of King's high school carpool.

In the fall of 1962, King began attending Lisbon High School in nearby Lisbon Falls, approximately six miles northeast of Durham. Because the town couldn't afford a school bus, they hired Mike's Taxi of Lisbon to transport the handful of kids to school.

The taxi, a converted hearse, carried King, the two Hall boys, Brian and Douglas, who lived down the street, and two girls, one of whom served as King's model for the character Carietta White (*Carrie*). Noted Brian Hall, when the limo arrived, there was a rush to get the best seat, because no one wanted to ride all the way to Lisbon with Carrie on his lap.

Carrie, who lived with her mother in a house down the street, was an odd girl, King remembers. One time, after doing lawn work for her mother, King went inside and was surprised to find the entire house a shrine to Jesus, filled with religious iconography. It made a deep impression on him; years later, the religious fanaticism of Carrie White's mother became a central theme in *Carrie*.

Recalled King, the real-world Carrie married a strange man who worked as a meteorologist and lived on the top of a nearby mountain. Together, they had several children. One day, for reasons unknown, she hung herself.

In *Carrie*, Carietta White suffers an untimely death, as well.

Lisbon Falls has changed little since King's day. The high school is still around, but a drive around town shows its scars. The local mill, an abandoned shoe factory, has been closed for decades, a reminder of Lisbon Falls' industrial past.

HERMON

In 1971, Stephen married Tabitha Jane Spruce, and the couple moved to Hermon, a small town west of Bangor. Like many small towns in Maine, Hermon seems untouched by time.

Then renting a double-wide mobile home on the side of a hill in Hermon, the Kings' memories of the town are understandably tainted. It was financially a bleak time for the Kings. Stephen took a teaching job at Hampden Academy, and Tabitha worked at the Dunkin' Donuts on Main Street in Bangor.

Left: King was almost suspended from Lisbon High School for self-publishing The Village Vomit, a parody of the school newspaper. Right: The town of Hermon, where King spent some difficult years.

Years later, after King became famous, he gave an interview to *Playboy* (1983), in which he said, "Hermon, Maine, which if not the asshole of the universe, is at least within farting distance of it." After reading King's refreshingly candid comment, Hermon's town manager, Ethan W. Arnoff, fired off a letter to the local newspaper, the *Bangor Daily News*, and said huffily that plans for a Stephen King day were canceled, and that plans for the "King Museum, originally sited upon his old trailer pad, are terminated."

King, who was then vacationing in Bridgton, could not be reached for comment, but he made it clear in a June 22, 1983, letter to the editor of the *Bangor Daily News* that he had no love lost for Hermon:

> To the editor:
> You can please some of the people all of the time, and all of the people some of the time, but you can't please all of the people all of the time. Mark Twain, who never made it as far north as Hermon, said something like that.
>   The town manager of Hermon may want to erect a Mark Twain museum on

my old trailer pad, because he has never been there—if he had been, they would have to look for yet another writer. I dread to think what Mark Twain might have made of Hermon.

I've lived in Maine all of my life, and people who know me and know my work will know I've had very few bad things to say about my home state. In fact, I have found a fair number of good things to say.

In Hermon I was evicted from my home, harried by my landlord and someone shot my dog. My wife carried the poor mutt out of the back field with one leg hanging by a string.

I'm sure there are lots of good people in Hermon, but it's still never going to be one of my favorite places.

For King, the only good thing that came out of Hermon was a manuscript—a short story that, for lack of anything else to work on, he turned into a short novel. The novel was *Carrie*, and, after it sold in paperback, it carried King away from Hermon and out of the classroom, and allowed him to do what he felt he was born to do—write books.

NORTH WINDHAM

Leaving high school teaching behind him permanently in 1973, King moved his family to North Windham, near Sebago Lake, where he rented a summer house for the winter.

Able to write without the distractions of financial demons haunting him, and freed from the seemingly endless task of grading papers and preparing for the next day's classes as a high school English teacher, King's mind cleared. He was able to focus on his next novel, titled *Second Coming*, which would later be published as *'Salem's Lot*.

Living in North Windham, King saw *Carrie* published in hardcover in 1974. *Carrie* was the first book of five from Doubleday, books that laid the groundwork for his spooky reputation as America's best-loved literary boogeyman.

After a brief stay in Colorado—a much-needed change of scenery—the Kings returned to Maine in 1975. As Tabitha King explained in an introduction to the collector's edition of *Carrie*, "We were supposed to go to New York for a publication party but the fog socked in the Portland Jetport and so we drove to New Hampshire for the weekend—we already had a babysitter. We stopped for gas in Bridgton, where later on we lived for five years and had our youngest child [Owen]."

Located forty miles northwest of Portland, Bridgton—in the Western Lakes and Mountains region of Maine—remains a small town, with a population of only 3,521.

Flanked by Long Lake—so named because of its elongated shape, running north-south—Bridgton proved to be an idyllic setting for the King family.

In his introduction to *Night Shift*, his first collection of short fiction, King wrote: "My family and I live in a pleasant house beside a relatively unpolluted lake in Maine; last fall I awoke one morning and saw a deer standing on the back lawn by the picnic table. We have a good life."

The ranch house, the first house he owned, was purchased for $150,000. Its address: RFD #2, Kansas Road, Bridgton, Maine 04009. (Years later, in 1997, the house sold again, after being offered at $450,000. The Maine Star Realty, Inc., which handled its sale, hammered home its most salable feature: "King wrote here!" The copy read: "The sun shines all day on these 2.65 private acres at 'The Ledges.' The 250' of waterfront includes beach and deep water with a separate cover. The daylight Ranch has 5 bedrooms, 2 1/2 baths, fireplace, full basement [King's home office]/garage and separate 3 car garage with unfinished apartment above.")

The geographic backdrop to King's novella "The Mist," Long Lake, Bridgton, and Harrison—the town across Long Lake—are instrumental in setting up the nightmarish premise: After the freak storm, David Drayton, while shopping at the local Federal Foods Supermarket, watches a strange mist roll into town, which brings unspeakable monsters purportedly the product of military experiments gone awry at a nearby military installation. It was, folks whispered, the Arrowhead Project.

Wanting to write an English ghost story, King then moved the family to England for one year; but unable to start the ghost novel and not finding England to his liking, he returned to Maine after only three months and bought a home in Center Lovell, which he still owns today.

Back in Maine, King finished writing *Cujo*, a novel that his former college professor and critic Burton Hatlen termed one of King's most Maine novels, geographically set near Center Lovell. (When a BBC film crew shot a documentary on King, he gave them a tour of the local area, including the place that was described, word for word, in *Cujo*—the location of the garage owned by Joe Camber.)

In 1978, the Kings moved to a rented house in Orrington, where he commuted to Orono while serving a stint as a writer-in-residence. In Orrington, a strange burial ground located a stone's throw from their rented house inspired him to write *Pet Sematary*.

"The Mist," one of King's best-known novellas, is principally set in Bridgton at a Federal Foods Supermarket that is set upon by monstrosities emerging from a mist.

Above: The house the Kings rented in Orrington was right off of Route 15, a major highway that claimed the lives of many local families' pets—including Smucky, the King family cat—thus providing the inspiration for *Pet Sematary*. Opposite: The swing that appears in *Pet Sematary* on the grounds of the Kings' Orrington house.

ORRINGTON

As recounted by Dave Barry—a fellow member of The Rock Bottom Remainders, a band made up of best-selling authors who perform for charity—in *Mid-Life Confidential*: When Stephen King first met him, King put his face within inches of Barry's and said in a very loud voice, "So Dave Barry, where do you get your ideas?"

It is a writer's joke—the kind only another writer will find hilariously funny—but for King and other writers, it's the question the curious are most likely to ask. (In King's case, a close second is: So, Stephen King, what was your childhood like? In other words, what horrific experience made you a horror writer?)

Sometimes, as King has pointed out, the idea seems to come from nowhere; and at other times, its genesis is easily stated, as in the case of *Pet Sematary*.

If you look on a map of the greater Bangor area, you'll see the Penobscot River winding its way from north to south. Across the river, on Route 15, about five miles from the heart of Brewer—the city that looks across the Penobscot toward Bangor—you'll find Orrington.

If you're on the east side of the Penobscot and want to get to Bangor, you have one choice: Route 15. Winding its way through hilly terrain, this major access route to Bangor has laid claim to a large number of animals because the trucks travel fast and few brake for animals short of a moose.

In 1978 the Kings moved to Orrington, where they rented a two-story house that faced Route 15. It was a year of transition for King, who published *The Stand* and *Night Shift*, completing his contractual obligations with Doubleday, which freed him to go to Viking.

He commuted to the University of Maine at Orono for a one-year stint as its writer-in-residence, which gave King the opportunity to tell Tabitha, as he'd always wanted to, that he was "leaving for the office." For a writer used to working at home, it was a major change in lifestyle.

In early 1979, according to Douglas Winter's *Stephen King: The Art of Darkness*, a neighbor called him with bad news: the family pet, a cat named Smucky that belonged to his daughter Naomi, had been run over by a passing truck. Route 15 had claimed its latest victim.

King, a writer-in-residence at UMO from 1978 to 79, answers students' questions after class. (UMO yearbook)

King, who had written regularly about horror in all its dimensions, found it difficult to tell his daughter the truth. His initial impulse, he told Winter, was to simply say he "hadn't seen him around, but Tabby said no, that she had to have that experience. So I told her, and she cried and cried. . . ."

When it came time to bury Smucky, there was no question as to where the burial would take place: the "pet sematary," as the neighborhood kids spelled it, with a crude, homemade sign marking its location, behind a house on a hill north of King's house.

Smucky was buried and Naomi underwent the grieving process. A few days after the burial, King's storytelling machinery cranked up. What if the family cat was killed by a passing truck? And what if it came back fundamentally changed—and what if, the next time, it wasn't the family pet but a family member?

It was every parent's worst nightmare, envisioned by King as a modern day retelling of the classic horror story by W. W. Jacobs, "The Monkey's Paw," in which a dead son is horrifyingly brought back to life. But Jacobs chose not to speculate on what lay beyond. The story ends as the father makes a final wish and mercifully sends his son back to the grave.

King decided it was time to explore the ultimate taboo—the mysteries that surround death and dying. The result was *Pet Sematary*, one of King's most horrific novels, which he had no intention of publishing. It was too bleak, with real-world associations that colored the book for him.

But word got out that King had refused to publish a novel because it was too scary, even for him; and despite entreaties from his readers, King held fast, refusing to release it, until an old Doubleday contract intervened.

A detail from the *Pet Sematary* movie poster shows the fictional pet cemetery based on the real-life Orrington locale.

In exchange for *Pet Sematary*, King was able to recoup all the money held in reserve at Doubleday.

The pleasure at finally being free of that maddening situation was tempered by the emotional pain King felt when thinking about the book, because it opened doors he preferred to keep shut. *Pet Sematary*—an unflinching look at death and all its ramifications—was in King's mind somehow associated with the death of Charlotte Littlefield, who had taught with him at Hampden Academy. Though King never elaborated on the association, it was clear that the writing of *Pet Sematary* affected him personally, in a way that most of his other novels did not.

King loved Littlefield, he said, as much as he did his own mother. King, in fact, dedicated *Roadwork* to Littlefield. "So it hurts me to talk about it; it hurts me to think about it. *Pet Sematary* is the one book that I haven't reread—I never want to go back there again, because it is a real cemetery," he told Douglas Winter with finality. (Winter added that his was the last interview King would give on the book.)

Pet Sematary is the story of Dr. Louis Creed, a rationalist who runs a university infirmary (modeled after the University of Maine at Orono). A neighbor, Jud Crandall, takes the Creeds behind their rented house to show them the neighborhood "pet sematary," where the local children bury their beloved pets, claimed on a regular basis by the passing trucks that travel on the route that cuts through town (modeled, obviously, after Route 15).

On seeing the pet cemetery, Dr. Creed's daughter, Ellie, is frightened, but not for herself; she's afraid for Church, her pet cat, and rightly so. Church soon becomes yet another victim of the road and is buried at the "pet sematary."

Remembering what he had been told about the supposed life-restoring powers of the Indian Micmac burial ground, a skeptical Louis Creed buries Church; afterward, Church comes back to life but is fundamentally *changed*.

That should have been enough of a lesson for Louis Creed, but when Louis's

King no doubt drew inspiration from the Mt. Pleasant cemetery in Bangor.

two-year-old son Gage becomes the next victim of the road, the father makes the decision to bring his son back across the river Styx, which brings even more horrifying results.

As for the original "pet sematary," it no longer exists. The cemetery, started by Amy Stanchfield when she buried a family cat, took on a life of its own after King's novel was published. "It was pretty exciting," recalled Stanchfield, interviewed by the *Bangor Daily News*, "but I don't think anybody knew much about it being where it was. It was a weird feeling knowing it was about my backyard. I couldn't go back out there for quite a while."

Amy Stanchfield's older sister, Bethany, had made the original "pet sematary" sign, but she eventually took it down because she knew that souvenir hunters would take it. "When the book first came out," recalled Bethany, "it was like 'Hey, we did something to inspire Stephen King.'" But she added, "Sometimes, I really kind of regret it. People tromping out there over my pets, taking the markers that we left for them. Why can't they just leave things like that alone? . . . I feel bad about taking the sign [down], and I'd really like to leave it up, but I know that somebody would just take it."

Because Ludlow is a thinly disguised Orrington, the greater Bangor area figures prominently in the book. In fact, it's King's ability to weave real-world references into his books that give them verisimilitude:

·The Bangor International Airport: The Creeds had flown out from here to Chicago, for a Thanksgiving holiday.

·The Bangor Mall: This was where Ellie Creed saw a "skinny" Santa Claus.

·Holiday Inn: When the Goldmans came into town to attend Gage's funeral, they stayed at this chain hotel (located on Odlin Road).

·Mount Hope Cemetery: This was where Jud and Norma Crandall bought plots. It's also the on-location site where *Pet Sematary* was filmed, and Stephen King played the role of the minister presiding over the burial of Gage Creed.

Though the original "pet sematary" is no more, the novel, and the film based on the novel, remain; and Orrington, a small town that would have otherwise remained virtually unknown to the world, permanently lost its anonymity when King put it on his literary map.

UNIVERSITY OF MAINE AT ORONO

When King graduated from high school, he applied to two colleges and was accepted to both. The first choice, Drew University, was too expensive, so he enrolled as a freshman at the University of Maine at its campus in Orono, a small town just north of Bangor.

As a freshman, King had to stay in the dorms. His old fear—of not fitting in—resurfaced with a vengeance. For someone who had spent his teenage years in rural Maine, Orono wasn't much of an adjustment, unlike college life which was a stark contrast from his high school days in Lisbon Falls.

"There I was," King wrote in the campus newspaper, years later, "all alone in Room 203 of Gannett Hall, clean-shaven, neatly dressed, and as green as apples in August. Outside on the grass between Gannett and Androscoggin Hall there were more people playing football than there were in my hometown. My few belongings looked pitifully uncollegiate. The room looked mass-produced. I was quite sure my roommate would turn out to be some kind of a freako, or even

Above: King roomed at Gannett Hall as a freshman at the University of Maine. Below: A college-bound King probably took this road frequently during his four years at UMO.

UMO's mascot is the Black Bear.

worse, hopelessly more 'With It' than I. I propped my girl's picture on my desk where I could look at it in the dismal days ahead, and wondered where the bathroom was."

King recalled that when he went home, he "swaggered around," as if to show he was no longer a high school kid wet behind the ears but, instead, a college man. But when he returned to campus, he would, in his words, "promptly shrink back to three feet tall again."

During his freshman year, in Freshman Composition, King met the first of four professors that would take him seriously as a writer, although he had not yet published professionally. As oberved by another member of the English department, "Jim Bishop was the first person who Steve King met on campus who was responsive to his work."

Bishop's recollections of King as a freshman are positive. Sanford Phippen, in *Maine* magazine (Fall 1989) recounts Bishop's observations in "The Student King": "Steve was a nice kid, a good student, but never had a lot of social confidence. Even then, though, he saw himself as a famous writer and thought he could make money at it. Steve was writing continuously, industriously, and diligently. He was amiable, resilient, and created his own world."

Just as in Durham, when Chesley would go over to his friend's house to hear a young King show off his remarkable grasp of storytelling, King's ability to create his own fictional worlds and the serious intent with which he wrote made him stand out at UMO.

During King's first year, he tried his hand at a full-length novel. The book was *The Long Walk*, and although it would eventually see publication under his Richard Bachman pen name, the book, then submitted under his name to a first novel competition, failed to win, depressing the fledgling writer who lacked the confidence to resubmit to another house.

The Long Walk was put aside and King concentrated on his studies.

In his second year, King broke into print professionally, but not with a novel. "The Glass Floor," his first professional sale, was a short story for *Startling Mystery Stories* that earned him thirty-five dollars. But it was proof that he could write and publish professionally, though it wasn't exactly what you'd call a prestigious showcase; the magazine was printed on cheap pulp paper with lurid, glossy covers.

No matter. King had tasted first blood and liked it.

In his sophomore year, in Burton Hatlen's class, King was exposed to William Faulkner and John Steinbeck, both regional writers who staked claim to a uniquely

American brand of fiction. Faulkner explored small-town life from his vantage point in Oxford, Mississippi, and Steinbeck wrote about California, most notably Salinas Valley. (King would later collect first editions by both writers.)

In due course, King approached Hatlen and asked for his opinions on *The Long Walk*.

Hatlen took it home and submitted to King's storytelling magic. To his surprise, the novel was not only readable but good. "I brought it home and laid it on the dining room table. My then-wife picked it up and started reading it and couldn't stop. That was also my experience. The narrative grabbed you and carried you forward. That was what was most striking about *The Long Walk*—King had a fully developed sense of narrative and pace. It was there already. It was quite amazing to see that."

Had Hatlen read *The Aftermath*, which King wrote when he was sixteen, he would have seen that the narrative skills exhibited in *The Long Walk* were present in that work, too. Clearly, King could tell a story. Now, what he needed was to be taken seriously, encouraged, and assisted toward professional publication.

The Long Walk made the rounds in the English department. Ted Holmes, who was the first to read it, declared to Hatlen that a new fictional voice had been found. So encouraged, King took the manuscript to one of his other professors, Carroll E. Terrell, a respected scholar whose published work includes books about Louis Zukofsky, Basil Bunting, William Carlos Williams, and Ezra Pound.

Terrell read the manuscript carefully and made suggestions to King, who rejected the criticism and stuck to his guns. Years later, Terrell admitted that he had erred in assuming this was a first novel. "I am conscious now," he wrote in *Stephen King: Man and Artist*, "that I thought *The Long Walk* was a first novel. But I should have known that it could have been no such thing. No one could have written such a balanced and designed book without a lot of practice; not just aimless practice, but conscious and designed practice."

In King's junior year, King applied to, and was accepted for, Burton Hatlen's Contemporary Poetry class. (Another student, an intense young woman who took her poetry very seriously, wasn't accepted to the class—Tabitha Jane Spruce, the future Mrs. Stephen King.)

By then, Stephen King had become something of a campus institution. Towering six feet, four inches, with long hair and a beard, King stood out. A member of the student council, outspoken and articulate, adamantly opposed to the Vietnam War, and active in drama productions, King made the front cover of *The Maine Campus*.

Working at the library part-time, he began dating another student who worked in the stacks: Tabitha Jane Spruce, who grew up in nearby Old Town, and was working toward her history degree. Years later, the future Mrs. Stephen King wrote in *Murderess Ink* (1979) that when she brought her long-haired, bearded boyfriend home to meet her parents for the first time, what they remembered was the *The Maine Campus* cover photo of him taken by Frank Kadi. In the photo, he looks like a maniac, wielding a double-barreled shotgun which is pointed straight at the viewer. Tabitha's parents expressed reservations about the man with whom their daughter had become seriously involved, and based on the photo, who could have faulted them? He looks, in that photo, every bit as crazy as Charles Manson—a stark contrast to the clean-cut photo portrait from his high school yearbook taken just a few years earlier.

In his senior year, King spoke up, loud and clear, at a student-faculty meeting that had met to assess the curriculum. King spoke out against the policy in the English department of turning its nose up at popular literature, ignoring (in his mind) the rightful place of popular culture. Burton Hatlen explains:

> I remember a meeting in which the students and faculty got together to talk
> about the curriculum of the English department. Several people have a memory of
> Steve standing up at this meeting and denouncing the department because he

had never been able to read a Shirley Jackson novel in any of the courses he had taken. He criticized the curriculum and insisted on the value and importance of popular culture and mass culture, and people listened to him. It was an important moment. King wanted to conduct a special seminar on popular American fiction, which produced a crisis. Here was an undergraduate proposing to teach a course.

King's proposal was taken seriously and in fact he did teach the course, Popular Literature and Culture, with Graham Adams, a teacher in the English department, as its front man. (It was the first, and last, time an undergraduate taught a course at UMO.)

The next month, King began appearing in the pages of *The Maine Campus* with an opinion column, "King's Garbage Truck," so named because, as he pointed out, you'd never know what he'd throw in it.

King's student editor, David Bright, was impressed with the quality of the work and his ability to meet the deadline without fail, though usually at the last minute. "The guy is very prolific," Bright recalled. "He likes to write and is excellent at it. He'd come in and bang these pieces out. They'd be letter-perfect and he'd lay them on the desk."

The column, however, wasn't all that King banged out: he produced a torrent of works for college publications—stories and poetry in campus publications like *Moth*, *Onan*, and *Ubris*—and the ambitious but flawed unpublished novel, *Sword in the Darkness*, which made the rounds but failed to sell.

Student-teaching in Hampden, a small town south of Bangor, King worked toward his teaching certification, knowing that his best chance for gainful employment was the teaching profession, at least until his writing career took off, if it ever did.

Given his druthers, King would have preferred teaching elementary school, since he felt that some high school students lacked the motivation to be in school—external forces kept them there—but it was a moot point: The job market was tight and no teaching jobs were available.

After graduation, he took a job pumping gas at a station off Interstate 95, near Orono; and, although no longer a student, he still contributed to *The Maine Campus* with "Slade," a western story that showed a seldom seen humorous side to his writing.

Soon thereafter, King put his teaching certification to good use, at the very school where he had student-taught— Hampden Academy—but after *Carrie* sold in paperback, it freed him from teaching and allowed him to do what he had wanted to do since he was a young kid with a headful of stories: write book-length fiction for a living.

King hams it up for the Hampden Academy yearbook (1972).

photo by Frank Kad

Study, Dammit!!

Though King never returned to high school to teach, he would, in 1978–79, teach again at UMO, as a writer-in-residence; and, in 1996, be the subject of a weekend symposium, "Reading Stephen King," at which scholars around the country gathered to read their papers on the many facets of his work. To those critics, at least, King did become the bridge between popular and critical fiction—a goal King had set for himself.

In retrospect, UMO gave King what he needed at that time in his life: a sense of identity, a place to form his worldview, and expansion of his personal and professional horizons; and most importantly, a place where his writing was encouraged by his professors.

How important was UMO to King? If King hadn't attended UMO:

·He wouldn't have met Tabitha Jane Spruce. (Marrying her, he said, was the smartest thing he ever did.)

·He wouldn't have met Burton Hatlen, who would prove to be his main contact at the University, and the one who brought him back for the one-year writer-in-residence stint.

·He wouldn't have had the encouragement he needed as a fledgling writer to persevere, to refine his own unique vision, expressed in his distinctive prose.

UMO gave of itself to King . . . and King reciprocated.

In 1980, Stephen King donated a small fortune in original manuscripts—including his unpublished novels—to the Folger Library's Special Collections, at the urging of then curator Eric Flower. (The university appraised the entire collection at $14,000, not realizing that individual manuscripts would have commanded that valuation, if made available through dealers who traded in King collectibles.)

Years later, UMO gave honorary doctorate degrees to both Stephen and Tabitha

King, at a commencement ceremony addressed by Stephen King. In time, King gave back to the college again, with a generous endowment, which the university had hoped for ever since it was obvious that King was not only a success but, clearly, in terms of overall book sales, the most popular writer in book publishing history.

The endowment—a long time coming—was welcomed with open arms and sighs of relief. Unlike other endowments, from alumni donating generously only to athletic programs, the Kings opted to reward academic excellence: a promise of $4 million, to be paid out $1 million each year, for scholarships (named in honor of King's former creative writing teacher, Ted Holmes) and for teachers' salaries.

Their generous gift came at a time when the state had cut back on educational funding; the timing, the Kings said, was coincidental. At a press conference announcing the gift, Stephen King said:

> What I'm trying to do is give something back to the university. The University of Maine is a great campus. It has always been a great campus. It is the flagship campus of the university system in this state. Kids who come from Maine and go to college in Maine tend to stay in the state. Tabby and I did that, and in the years that we have lived here, we've paid literally millions of tax dollars in state income tax. Anybody in government, state or otherwise, who suggests that there's a dichotomy between balancing the budget here in Maine and funding education is just flat wrong.
>
> Good education is good business, and there's no argument about that. I only say that because we can't do this by ourselves and wouldn't want to. The university belongs to everyone in Maine, and it's everyone's responsibility. I hope that people who agree that this is a worthwhile institution will talk to their state legislators and talk to Governor King. Write these people letters, call them on the phone, send faxes and say "turn around, reevaluate your position concerning higher education in this state." Do it now and let's get back into the business of educating Maine boys and girls in Maine.
>
> I came to the University of Maine and graduated from the University of Maine because of the scholarship help that I received. My mother was a housekeeper and made about $5,000 a year. There was no way I could have afforded a college education without help.

To which Tabitha King added: "I was one of eight children and there was simply no money for college. I worked, as Steve did, and I obtained some scholarship help that saw me through."

OLD TOWN

Located north of Orono, Old Town is where Tabitha King grew up. Not surprisingly, Tabitha King has given back to the community that sustained her for so many years, notably to the town's library, which named its new wing after her, the Tabitha Jane Spruce King Wing.

Above: The Old Town Public Library honors Mrs. King's philanthropy with a Tabitha Jane Spruce King Wing. Below: Tabitha King's hometown of Old Town is just north of Bangor and Orono.

INSIDE MAGAZINE: *Why do you stay in Maine?*

KING: *I'm a hick.*

INSIDE: *There really isn't anything here.*

KING: *That's one of the reasons I like it in Bangor; if someone wants to get to me, they really have to be very dedicated. . . . I grew up here. I went to one-room schoolhouses. There were outhouses. I am a hick and this is where I feel at home.*

CHAPTER 2: BANGOR—STEPHEN'S KINGDOM

J ust before the turn of the century, Bangor (the Queen city—as Mainers call it) was known for its chief export—the prized white pine, which was shipped all over the world. As Zeis and Zoldis recount in *Woodsmen and Whigs: Historic Images of Bangor, Maine*, "Bangor's lumber exports peaked in 1872, when almost 250 million board feet were shipped from the port. Because of the tremendous volume of lumber that left the city on ships, Bangor became known as the 'Lumber Capital of the World.' The harbor and its surrounding neighborhoods bustled with activity; between 1860 and 1872 an average of more than 2,200 ships entered the harbor each year. Today, Bangor shows little evidence of the once thriving industry. The waterfront is quiet, woodsmen and sailors no longer roam the streets, sawmills are gone, and the boarding houses, hotels, bars, and houses of pleasure have been torn down."

In fact, the only surviving symbols of the old Bangor can be found not on the waterfront but on Main Street and West Broadway.

On Main Street: Outfitted in traditional lumberjack clothing—L.L. Bean comes readily to mind—a thirty-two-foot tall Paul Bunyan, axe in hand, looks east beyond Main Street and toward the Penobscot River that separates Bangor from Orrington.

The only other evidence of the old ways can be found on West Broadway, where the lumber barons built their palatial homes at the turn of the century. Now part of the

Above: At the turn of the century West Broadway was lined with the palatial homes of Bangor's lumber barons. The William Arnold house (foreground, left), built in 1856, is now home to the Kings.

town's Historic District, the houses are all charming, but one house in particular stands out. It used to be known as the William Arnold House, named after its builder, not a lumber baron but a "prosperous livery stable owner," according to Deborah Thompson, author of *Bangor, Maine, 1769–1914, An Architectural History.*

The house, the author points out, was the first to be built on the street. Completed in 1856, Arnold's house—still one of the most distinctive on the street—was valued at six thousand dollars. "It's an Italianate villa with asymmetrical massing, a square-hipped roof and a finialed tower," Terry Steel explains, noting that, "A smaller, octagonal tower is a later addition in the Queen Anne style of the 1880s and 90s." (Steel ought to know. He's an architectural blacksmith who built the elaborate wrought-iron fence around the house.)

The distinctive house would catch anyone's attention, but one admirer in particular felt drawn to it. The *Bangor Daily News* notes:

Paul Bunyan keeps watch over Bangor, once known as the "Lumber Capital of the World."

> As a girl she strolled down West Broadway with a friend and dreamed of living in one of the mansions. She leaned toward the red one with towers. She certainly never thought she'd live there one day.
>
> But the wide-eyed girl grew up to be author Tabitha King and married the man who became the most famous horror author of our time, Stephen King.

Regarding the house, replete with towers and secret passages, Tabitha remarked, "I thought it was destiny." It may very well be destiny, because Bangor seems like a perfect fit for the Kings. As King told an interviewer in *Bare Bones*, "Bangor, Maine . . . is not a town calculated to make anybody feel famous. The only claim to fame is a big plastic statue of Paul Bunyan. You just live there and keep your head down."

Above: A bird's eye view of the Kings' sprawling house reveals its numerous renovations and additions, including the indoor swimming pool which juts out from the lower left.
Opposite: Tabitha and Stephen in front of their dream house, circa 1980. (Photo courtesy of the *Bangor Daily News*)

THE WILLIAM ARNOLD HOUSE

The Kings were looking for a winter home and found their dream house: an Italianate villa, which the Kings bought in 1980 for the bargain price of $135,000.

Naturally, the Kings made extensive renovations to the house, since it not only had to serve as home for a family of five but also as a functioning home office for two working writers. (Tabitha King, in 1981, published *Small World*, a novel dedicated to "the Boogeyman, with love" and has gone on to publish several more novels since then at NAL.)

It took four years to make the renovations, but when completed, the house was very livable indeed: a front porch and a carriage port had been added, but the centerpiece was the indoor pool, which juts out from the back of the house—not that you'd know it's there, since it's difficult to see from the gates that surround the twenty-three room house.

A three-headed griffin guards the King residence.

In fact, passersby get a forced perspective of the house, a front-on look restricted by two rows of five-foot-high shrubbery. (An aerial view best shows off the house, for its siting prevents adequate viewing from all vantage points on the ground.)

In the beginning, the Kings optimistically hoped that there'd be no need for barricading themselves behind a fence, to protect themselves from the intrusiveness of tourists or, worse, from the creepazoids that plagued them; but it soon became apparent that King's fame and notoriety was too big a draw for his devoted fans, as was the distinctive house itself. A discreetly posted sign near the doorbell made it clear that because the Kings were writers who worked at home, they could not come to the door to answer questions or sign books; the passive approach, they soon learned, didn't dissuade the determined.

A fence, they realized, would have to go up around the property; and to build the fence, they retained the services of Terry Steel, one of the few architectural blacksmiths in the country, whom they knew from Center Lovell.

As for the fence, form would follow function, so the Kings, after extensive consultation with Steel, envisioned a wrought-iron fence that clearly said, in unmistakable visual language: Look all you want, but don't even think of trespassing.

Observed Steel, "the commission took a year-and-a-half to finish—270 lineal feet of hand-forged fence, weighing 11,000 pounds, punctuated by two gates composed of spiders, webs, goat heads, and winged bats. The editor of the local paper called the project a major contribution to the architecture of the city of Bangor. A neighbor comes over to tell me the fence is 'just what the house needed,' and turns to eye her own front yard. One thing's for sure. Anyone touring Bangor trying to pick out the house where Stephen King lives will have little trouble finding it."

"K" for King lets tourists know they've come to the right house.

Originally, the fence did not completely encircle the house, since Stephen King felt that he didn't want to barricade himself behind it. Unfortunately, as the years passed, and as King's fame grew, the gates—to the Kings' dismay—had to be locked and, in time, the house became such a tourist magnet that the fence would have to encircle the entire property.

West Broadway, about a mile from Sanford Street, where the Kings once rented a second-story walk-up, used to be a quiet, residential street, but the presence of Stephen King transformed it into a year-round attraction.

The local residents live with it—none seem to complain—but at Halloween, the steady stream of people becomes a raging torrent, too obvious to ignore. For the first few years that they lived in the mansion, the Kings gave out treats for Halloween, usually running out several times in the course of the evening, requiring multiple

A custom-designed wrought iron fence surrounds 47 West Broadway, leaving no mystery as to which house belongs to the Kings. (Photo by Caroll Hall, courtesy of the *Bangor Daily News*)

trips to the grocery store to replenish the candy supply.

The house was unofficially known as "spook central," said King, and it just didn't feel like Halloween if you didn't get a treat from the Boogeyman of Bangor. (In the spirit of things, King once installed an in-ground speaker on his property, which emitted the most ghastly sounds as the kids made their way to the front porch—the trick was on the trick-or-treaters.)

Predictably, the crowds grew larger every year, requiring the police for traffic control, at which point the Kings realized it was best to spirit themselves away for the holiday.

For some years now, the Kings have run a small display ad in the local paper right before Halloween stating that they will be gone, to dissuade the locals and the media

On Halloween, local spooks wait patiently for their turn to trick-or-treat at Spook Central. (Photo courtesy of the *Bangor Daily News*)

from converging on Ghost Central. (Those who do show up will find a dimly lit house and the gate barred.)

But even the fence and the prominently posted signs dissuading trespassers weren't enough to deter the genuine nutcases, as the Kings later found out. In two instances, out-of-towners haunted Bangor and, specifically, the Kings' home. A California man set up his dilapidated van next to Betts Bookstore on Main Street and loudly proclaimed his theory that Stephen King killed John Lennon, and that the government was helping King cover it up. And in one horrific incident, when Tabitha King was home alone, one of the more determined—and admittedly unbalanced—brazenly broke into the house through the kitchen window. He confronted Tabitha King and told her he had a homemade bomb, and showed it to her. (The bomb was later proven to be fake—a handful of wires and switches on a decorated box—but at the time, it seemed real enough.)

Any illusions that the Kings had about the pressing need to beef up security were now dispelled. Soon after that nightmarish situation—something straight out of a King novel—prominent signs were posted, closed-circuit television cameras that scanned the grounds were strategically sited, the front gate was locked, and the driveway sported a Doorking, a numerical keypad entry device. Driven by necessity, the Kings had to barricade themselves in their own castle, now under year-round siege.

Though the augmented security measures have deterred the fanatical from scaling the fence and attempting another break-in, it doesn't deter

Tabitha and Stephen discuss the break-in bomb scare with the local press in April, 1981, remarking that they are a "lightning rod" for obsessed fans. (Photo courtesy of the *Bangor Daily News*)

the tour buses that pull over on a side road near West Broadway. Spilling out like ants from an anthill, dozens of camera-equipped celebrity seekers want photographic evidence that they've been to the house that put Bangor on the literary map.

King hadn't realized how bad it had gotten, until one day, when he took the family dog—a Welsh Corgi named Marlowe—out for a pit stop, he heard the distinctive click-click of camera shutters. To his horror, he saw dozens of tourists taking pictures of his dog evacuating its bowels. It was one thing when fans stalked him with cameras . . . but his dog?

So far as King was concerned, it was not the time to shoot a Kodak moment, but the celebrity-starved tourists obviously felt differently, so King did what anyone else would have done: He installed a row of hedges, obscuring most of the yard from frontal view. Now, at least, Marlowe would have a little privacy.

Little by little, the tourists, fans, and nutcases forced the Kings to do the very thing they didn't want to do: turn a private home into an electronically guarded fortress of solitude.

Building a baseball field is more work than you might imagine. I laid out a whole field, but it was there in spirit only. . . . My intuition told me that it was the grass that was important. It took me three seasons to hone that grass to its proper texture, to its proper color.

—*Shoeless Joe*, by W. P. Kinsella

Above: The Shawn Trevor Mansfield Baseball Complex takes shape. (Photo courtesy of the *Bangor Daily News*)
Left: King, described by biographer Douglas Winter as a "baseball junkie," is a devoted Red Sox fan. (Photo courtesy of the *Bangor Daily News*)

THIS BASEBALL FIELD
IS DEDICATED TO THE
MEMORY OF
SHAWN TREVOR MANSFIELD
AND ALL THE OTHER KIDS
WHO DIDN'T HAVE A CHANCE
TO PLAY.

DEDICATED JUNE 1, 1992

THE SHAWN TREVOR MANSFIELD BASEBALL COMPLEX

King's field of dreams—understandably nicknamed by locals as the "field of screams"—took root in 1989, when David Mansfield, coach of the Bangor West Little League team, called on the players' parents to lend a hand working on the run-down ballfield behind Bangor's Coca-Cola plant. Stephen King came to help—his then twelve-year-old son Owen was the first baseman—and, according to sportswriter Bob Haskell (of the *Bangor Daily News*), the germ of the idea presented itself. Recalled King, "We were out there in the mud. It was an impossible job. So I said, 'Let's build a Cadillac field that everybody can play on above Little League.'"

Bangor West, under Mansfield's coaching, went on to win the state championship that year—an odyssey captured in print by King in "Head Down" (published in *The New Yorker* and reprinted in *The Best American Sports Writing 1991*).

After the season ended, King's vision took concrete form when he magnanimously ponied up the $1.2 million to build the field and gave it to the city. He recommended that the new field be called the Shawn Trevor Mansfield Baseball Complex, named

Above left: King's "field of screams" is dedicated to Shawn Trevor Mansfield. Above right: King winds up for the pitch. (Photo courtesy of the *Bangor Daily News*)

Measuring 330 feet down the foul lines, this first-rate field has all the attributes of a professional park, with the exception of a press box.

after Dave Mansfield's son who died at the age of fourteen of cerebral palsy.

For those who know King, the gift came as no surprise, because the Kings—in ways large and small, publicly and anonymously—have given generously of their time, effort, and money to the local and surrounding communities. But long before the Kings had the wherewithal to make such generous donations, Stephen King enjoyed a lifelong love affair with baseball that began when he was just a kid. "Baseball," wrote Bob Haskell, "has been [King's] oasis and his escape for more than thirty years—since marveling over Don Larsen's perfect game during the 1956 World Series that he watched on a tiny black-and-white television when he was nine and living with his mother in Stratford, Connecticut." As Haskell writes, King "is a baseball junkie."

King's interest is not restricted to Little League ball; he is, in fact, a big fan of the perenially disappointing Boston Red Sox, a team that hasn't won a World Series since 1926. (Hope springs eternal.) He has season tickets for the Red Sox, and, like any other fan, he sits in the bleachers with his hot dog and drink in hand and yells at the players on the field. (During one such incident, with biographer Douglas Winter present, after King called Red Sox Steve Kemp a bum, the man seated in front of King turned around and suggested King put him in one of his novels, not realizing that King had already done so, in *Cujo*.)

Clockwise from left: P. J. Doure, Nicholas Larochelle, Greg Treadwell, Michael Larochelle, and Alex McManus are some of the local youths who enjoy the Mansfield Baseball Complex.

Closer to home, King's thoughts turn to Little League, although there is nothing little about his thoughts on how a Little League ballfield ought to look. As sportswriter Bob Haskell notes in the *1992 Complete Handbook to Baseball* the field is first-rate, sporting a professional lighting system, a computer-controlled sprinkler system to water the 115,000 square feet of Kentucky bluegrass sod, a drainage system so the field won't remain soaked after a hard rain, bleachers that seat 1,500 spectators, and two hundred tons of Georgia clay on a field that runs 330 feet down the foul lines. The only omission, by design: a press box, which King considered a low priority. The money, King said, would be spent on the essentials, like the field itself. No matter: the fans cheering in the bleachers never noticed the absence of a press box; what they did care about was that, for the first time, Bangor has a first-rate ballfield, instead of its underwhelming predecessor, which King described to Daniel Goldin of the *Boston Globe* as a "sad, neglected, overgrown, frost-heaved, guilty afterthought."

For King, though, the field is more than what it appears to be for its many fans. Talking about his adopted city in an interview with the *Globe*, King explained, "There was a time before baseball when I was kind of an isolated guy. I was in the [Bangor] community, but I didn't belong to the community . . . . I paid my dues. I'm in without buying my way in. The field is my way of saying, "The trial marriage is over. I'm here, and I'm staying."

King continually gives back to Bangor, the town he calls home.

King originally bought WZON to ensure that there is always hard rock on the airwaves. (It now has an all-sports format.)

King's link with the station produced an appropriately eerie T-shirt.

I did it because the cutting edge of rock and roll has grown dangerously blunt in these latter days.

—Stephen King, on why he bought WZON

WZON

As King tells it, in "Between Rock and a Soft Place," a piece he wrote for *Playboy* magazine, he had rented a car at Boston's Logan Airport to get him home, and on that long, lonely drive up the interstate, he "wanted to dial some good rock 'n' roll and turn the volume up until the speakers started to distort."

Unfortunately, as he twisted the dial from the low to the high end of the A.M. bandwidth, he found to his horror that there were no hard rock stations on the air. "That was when I began to worry—to seriously worry—about rock 'n' roll," he wrote.

That thought must have been in his mind when Arthur Greene, his business manager, recommended he make some business investments and let his money work for him.

King thought about it, figured it was a good idea, and decided to invest in his own backyard. He soon discovered that an A.M. radio station, WZON, was up for sale. (A WZON staffer suggested he buy it.)

Originally WACZ—before that, in 1926, it was WLBZ—Stephen King renamed it WZON, operated by the Zone Corporation, so named after his novel, *The Dead Zone*.

As a business investment, the station was marginal; and in early 1988, King made the decision to sell it after he saw its ratings fall and its profits decline. As King pointed out to the *Bangor Daily News*, he was willing to make an investment, but not to continually bleed money.

But WZON did provide one major benefit to King: He could turn on the radio and sit down to write, knowing that he'd like the music—the outrageously loud, head-banging music that dissuades people from approaching him while he is writing.

General Manager Chris Spruce in the booth at WKIT/WZON.

By late 1988, King decided not to sell, after all, preferring instead to change the format. The station's ownership would change from the Zone Corporation to a not-for-profit corporation, the Bangor Public Communications, Inc., with King as its president.

The Stephen King newsletter *Castle Rock* reported that "the station currently offers classic and album rock, mixed with blues, as its basic format. However, listeners also are apt to hear some crossover country songs and an occasional heavy metal tune as part of the station's varied format. Plans are being made to add other types of music to the programming, including special blocks of gospel and New Age music." Times change, and with it, so did the format of WZON.

In recent years, WZON has changed from the Dead Zone to the Sports Zone. Dale Duff, the station's program director, wrote on his "Duffel Bag" page on the station's website that "The winter broadcast schedule is jam-packed with University of Maine hockey and basketball; plenty of high school basketball and hockey; and don't forget the Bruins and the Celtics."

Eastern Maine's only all-sports station current weekday schedule includes such nationally syndicated shows as *The Fabulous Sports Babe*, *The Tony Kornheiser Show*, and *The "Papa Joe" Cavalier Show*.

The station offers a wide assortment of promotional tie-in clothing, including boxer shorts, which were likely inspired by Bob Haskell, a *Bangor Daily News* sportswriter who gamely bet King about his beloved Red Sox and lost, forcing him to wear his skivvies in public and eat symbolic crow in the form of chicken, while King, dressed in a tuxedo, fed him his fowl dish. (If you're ever in Bangor and see Bob Haskell, tell him that WZON is now selling boxers, and he'd better stock up before the next Red Sox season.)

As for rock and roll fans who lament the loss of WZON's rocking status, take heart: Tune in to 100.6 on the A.M. dial to WKIT, a hard-rocking station owned by—you guessed it—Stephen King.

STEPHEN KING'S OFFICE

As King soon realized, it was one thing to have a home office for himself and Tabitha, but quite another to have his secretarial staff working out of the same house. At first, it wasn't much of an imposition; after all, his secretary was Tabitha's sister, Stephanie Leonard, whose husband worked as their groundskeeper and mechanic. But as the professional demands on King grew—the ever-increasing number of phone calls and letters—Shirley Sonderegger was hired to help Stephanie with the workload.

In time, it became apparent that having a staff in the house for eight hours every day during the workweek meant that there was no privacy until the weekend, so the Kings looked around Bangor to find a suitable location for an office.

The office location is an open secret around town, but because it would draw tourists like the Kings' home on West Broadway, its address is not listed in any civic directory, nor is the office phone number listed in the phone directory. In other words, it's a private office and the tour buses should go elsewhere. (After the break-in at the King house, the office was also outfitted with closed-circuit television cameras, ensuring that only the recognized can get in.)

According to David Lowell, who has been to the office, its interior looks pretty much like any other office—a complement of secretaries, office equipment, and a lot of activity during banker's hours—but the memorabilia on the walls makes it clear it's Stephen King's domain.

As to its location: I seem to remember that it's on the outskirts of Bangor, near the Penobscot River . . . no, wait, I think it's in the downtown area, not far from Betts Bookstore. (Hey, don't *you* remember? Where'd you put that map?)

PHILTRUM PRESS

Unless you were one of the lucky few, you missed out on a King book, *Six Stories*—a collection of six short works of fiction, including two new tales. The book contains "Lunch at the Gotham Café" (from *Dark Love*), "L.T.'s Theory of Pets" (a new story), "Luckey Quarter" (from *USA Weekend*), "Autopsy Room Four" (a new story), "Blind Willie" (from *Anateus*), and the 1994 O. Henry Award winner, "The Man in the Black Suit" (from *The New Yorker*).

A trade paperback of 197 pages, the book costs $80, and demand was so high that it sold out well before publication. The book is now selling for $400, if you can find a copy.

Six Stories was published by King's own Philtrum Press.

So, you wonder, what makes it so special? Several things: first, it's by Stephen King; second, it's from Philtrum Press, his own private press; third, it showcases two new stories; and, fourth, it's signed and numbered by King, in an edition of only 1,100 copies, of which only 900 were offered for sale to the general public. Welcome to the world of specialty publishing, small presses, and in particular, Stephen King's private publications.

Begun in 1982 to issue King's Christmas greetings—installments of a novel in progress, *The Plant*, published as pamphlets—Philtrum Press has also issued other works by King, and a book by Don Robertson. The press's design work is handled by Michael Alpert, who went to college with King, and the printing is "cared for" by the Stinehour Press in nearby Lunenberg, Vermont.

To date Philtrum has published three installments of *The Plant* in 1982, 1983, and 1985 (a set of all three costs $3,000); *The Eyes of the Dragon* in 1984 (illustrated by Kenny Ray Linkous, the book was sold for $120 so King could afford to give away copies to people on his Christmas greetings list, which made this a break-even project); and in 1987, both limited and trade editions in hardcover of *The Ideal, Genuine Man* by Don Robertson, a writer whom King read as a teenager and whose work he openly admires.

Using a post office box as its "front" office, Philtrum Press maintains no mailing list, sends no announcements of forthcoming projects, and publishes sporadically, which is just what King had in mind. In other words, it doesn't operate like any other small press.

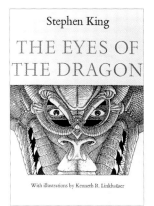

The Eyes of the Dragon, published by Philtrum Press, is a collector's item.

Obviously, if King so chose, Philtrum could be a big operation indeed, a self-publishing/promotion venue for him that, in scope and size, would rival Anne Rice's impressive offerings from her website, with its variety of official merchandising. But King has deliberately chosen a low profile for his company that publishes only when the need arises, usually every few years.

In his introduction to Robertson's *The Ideal, Genuine Man*, King wrote: "There are people who love the industry, but I am not one of them. . . . We have a staff of five, although I (as president) and Stephanie Leonard (treasurer and my sister-in-law) are contemplating adding a temp to deal with mail orders. We are, in other words, a very humble storefront in a world dominated by a few great glassy shopping malls."

Philtrum is a humble operation, but its first-class publications—beautifully designed and typeset, on heavy paper stock, and sturdily bound—show just how beautiful books can be when they receive the care and attention they deserve.

BETTS BOOKSTORE

For many years, the philosophy among the small, independent bookstores was "build it and they will come." In those days, the superstores—the gargantuan bookstore/eatery/reading libraries such as Borders and Barnes & Noble—hadn't assumed their Borg-like position in the marketplace, assimilating the smaller stores' hard-earned customer base with the wider selection and discounted prices that the independents can't afford to provide.

If that weren't bad enough, the book trade saw the marketplace further crowded with warehouse discounters that offered up to 40 percent off a handful of best-sellers, eroding the independents' book sales. In order to survive, some independents specialized. They offered what the larger stores could not, explored a niche too small for larger stores to exploit, and supplemented the retail presence with mail-order and Internet sales.

In 1988, when I began researching the first edition of *The Stephen King Companion*, I was surprised that no bookstore in Bangor catered to King fans. Surely the local community could support it, especially if supplemented with a mail-order operation. Other mail-order specialty dealers selling King collectibles did well, so why hadn't anyone in Bangor thought to specialize in things King for their needful things?

Stuart and Penney Tinker, longtime readers-turned-booksellers, had wondered the same thing; and after doing their homework, they realized that the most obvious market niche in town was going unfilled.

Wanting to buy a brand-name bookstore, the Tinkers bought Betts Bookstore— a permanent fixture since 1938 in the downtown Bangor area, conveniently located to shoppers.

Above: Stuart Tinker— along with his wife, Penney—fill the niche of "all things King" with Betts Bookstore.

They wisely stocked up on King books—both Stephen's and Tabitha's—and the word slowly went out: If you want to buy anything by either Stephen or Tabitha King, your best bet is Betts Bookstore.

The early years were rough, as they are for any start-up. As Stuart recalled, "Since we were starting out with no experience and no money, we really struggled, and Steve knew it. He agreed to do a book signing—his first locally in six years. Afterward, he came into the store on a regular basis and did what he could to help us get the store up and running."

In addition to stocking the current books in print, Stuart Tinker also carries Stephen King collectibles. Stuart discovered, as have many specialty booksellers, that King's customer base is large enough to support a thriving collector's market that eagerly snaps up every signed limited edition, usually before publication. In fact, they also buy books about King, many of which are also published in limited editions.

The store's mail-order business mushroomed, taking on a life of its own. Tinkers' mailing now numbers more than four thousand hardcore King fans.

Unlike some of the other specialty booksellers—here today, gone tomorrow—the

Tinkers have staying power and, instead of getting squeezed out by the Borders superstore near the Bangor Mall and the nearby Sam's Club that offers each new King book heavily discounted, the Tinkers have thrived. Betts Bookstore is, in the minds of King fans worldwide, the place to go to sell or buy anything related to King. Betts devotes its front section to things King, from the affordable (inexpensive trade paperbacks) to the spectacularly priced: at the time of this book's publication, $995 for a signed, numbered edition of *The Stand*, the book King's fans cite as their all-time favorite. (Never mind that it originally cost $325. A grand book in its own right, it's bound in black leather, the text is printed in two colors, and the book itself is laid in a red-velvet-lined, coffin-like black box with a lid. It is, no question, one hell of a beautiful book.)

If you're a King collector, going into Betts Bookstore is like going into the fabled Aladdin's Cave of Treasures. The difference, of course, is that the treasures in Betts are all for sale; and, for the

Betts Bookstore is like Aladdin's Cave of Treasures for King collectors.

investment-minded, keep in mind that King collectibles have more than held their own in value, increasing dramatically in value, and have proven to have high liquidity.

Of course, the Tinkers regularly update the list of King books for sale—at the time of this book's publication *Six Stories* is $400, but there's even more expensive fare, if you're so inclined: for $5,000, a set of matching numbered copies of the first four *Dark Tower* novels, and thrown in for good measure a matching numbered copy of *Desperation*.

Two needful things for sale at Betts: on the left is a brass ornament of the Kings' house and on the right an ornament promoting Derry, Maine—the fictional town based on Bangor that sets the stage for several of King's books.

But not everything is priced only for collectors. You can get a wooden ornament in the shape of Maine, with Derry marked on it; or, if you want something a little more elegant, a brass ornament in the shape of the King house.

Regardless of whether you shop at the store, buy from the catalog, or browse the store's website, here's my advice to you: Yield to temptation—it may not come your way again. (Do so, at least, on your birthday; be good to yourself.) At the very least, if you hunger for a King collectible, you can window-shop at the store itself or feast your eyes on its website.

At the Bangor Public Library, the Tile Wall lists everyone who contributed to the fund-raising effort. (Tabitha and Stephens' names are inscribed on the second tile from the bottom.)

A library card is a ticket to a thousand universes.
There's so much more inside the walls than I can imagine.

—Tabitha King quoted in "City Buries Time Capsule," by Ruth-Ellen Cohen, *Bangor Daily News* (May 4, 1998)

THE BANGOR PUBLIC LIBRARY

The long-awaited rededication day for the Bangor Public Library dawned with overcast skies—eerily reminiscent of a Stephen King novel. They soon cleared, and a crowd of 250, including Stephen and Tabitha King, assembled on the grounds of the Bangor Public Library off Harlow Street to watch the burial of a time capsule containing more than two hundred artifacts from local residents.

Before the capsule was lowered, Stephen King literally made his mark on history, on the time capsule itself, on which he wrote: "Hello from the 20th century," and signed his name with his distinctive scrawl. According to the *Bangor Daily News*, King told a young boy who witnessed his signing, "You can tell your grandchildren: 'I was the last person to see that. . . .'"

The TimeStoppers-brand time capsule—a white, barrel-shaped object—was then ceremoniously lowered into the ground by two sixth-graders, Caitlin Edward and Erin McLean, beneath the patio by the Children's Room. It will be excavated in 2046 by future sixth-graders.

It was a fitting, ceremonial end to a fund-raising program that began on a sour note in 1993 when Dan Wellington, Bangor's Code Enforcement Officer, called a librarian "asking if the library wanted to close down the front steps on its own or have Code Enforcement do the job. The library agreed to close the west side of the front steps, knowing that the east side and the children's entrance steps were also wobbly and falling inward. Soon after the yellow tape and sawhorses blocked off the offending area, author Tabitha King was sitting in the Director's office asking what she and Stephen could do to help," noted Michael Alpert in *Seven Books in a Footlocker* (1998), a commemorative book tied into the fund-raising effort.

The first step was to assess the extent of damages to the structure itself, so the Kings funded an engineering study done by a local company, which revealed the extent of the problems: " . . . the antiquated wiring and plumbing, the numerous code violations, and the dangerous conditions of the front steps."

Because the funding for the library was earmarked only for books and salaries, but not for the upkeep of the building itself, the only solution was to mount a major fundraising effort, which hadn't been done since before the turn of the century. The targeted amount: $8.5 million.

Setting the example, Stephen and Tabitha King got the fund-raising off to a brisk start at its Campaign Kickoff by making a pledge of $2.5 million if the city would match it, which it did unanimously. The remaining $3.5 million was to come from the citizens.

Having written a large check, the Kings could have justifiably said they had paid more than their fair share and left it at that, but instead they rolled up their sleeves with the other Bangorites and got to work. For the Kings, it became what Tabitha termed their pet project.

Tabitha chaired the Executive Committee overseeing the fund-raising effort, and Stephen was directly involved in fund-raising: he gave a sold-out reading at the Bangor Auditorium that drew thousands of people, allowed the library to sell videotapes of the talk, and appeared on *Jeopardy* as a celebrity guest to raise additional money. As recounted in *Seven Books in a Footlocker*, other Bangor citizens pitched in and helped where they could, in ways large and small. George Mason, a Maine artist, was commissioned to design a "Tile Wall," a row of bricks on which was carved the name of each contributor, to be inset in the library wall. (The Kings share the same tile as the *Bangor Daily News*, positioned halfway down on the wall's left side.)

It seems fitting that, in addition to the tile, the Kings were honored in *Seven Books in a Footlocker*, with a remembrance from their longtime friend and Philtrum Press designer Michael Alpert:

> Libraries exist because there are writers and there are readers. Tabitha and Stephen King are, first of all, committed writers. They are also voracious readers. And the Kings have long been community leaders, library fans, and benefactors. During the complex process of renovating and expanding the Bangor Public Library, the Kings' involvement in time and financial donations has been crucial.

On its rededication day, Tabitha King echoed Alpert's observations. This project, she told the hometown newspaper, brought her "huge satisfaction. It came closest to what Stephen and I have done with both our professional lives, in terms of what's important to us."

The end result, noted the *Bangor Daily News*: " . . . a building filled with light, with calm, inviting colors, and something interesting to see on every side. They [the patrons] found plenty of room to sit and enjoy a book or a magazine and what appeared to many as miles of open stacks. Twenty-one computers with access to the Internet were available for the public. Additional terminals for the library's catalog were spread throughout the building. More importantly, the dignity of the original building was retained."

In *Insomnia*, abortion-rights activist Susan Day is scheduled to speak at the Civic Center in King's fictional town of Derry, Maine.

As longtime King fans know, Derry was put on the map by King when he moved to Bangor and wanted to write a long novel set in a Maine city. That novel was *IT* and Bangor became Derry.

The Bangor Civic Center and Auditorium on Main Street has hosted King twice. In 1985, King gave a three-hour talk/reading, an "Evening with Stephen King," to raise money for the Bangor library drive; and four years later, King was instrumental in getting his fellow band members to put on a Rock Bottom Remainders concert, to raise money for the Shaw House, a temporary shelter for homeless teens.

An Evening with Stephen King

Going the route of Mark Twain, King has amply proven his ability to speak extemporaneously, and entertainingly, at length, to capacity crowds, offering anecdotes, jokes, commentary, and a reading from his own texts. (If you've never been able to attend one of his talks, you've missed a real treat. You owe it to yourself to buy one of his books on tape with himself as the reader.)

Over the years, King has spoken to numerous library groups, both in and out of state (Billerica, MA; Virginia Beach, VA; and Truth or Consequences, NM, to name but a few). And he's also spoken at numerous bookstores, most notably on a coast-to-coast tour to support *Insomnia*, during which he rode coast to coast on his Harley, visiting hand-picked independent booksellers: Northshire Bookstore (Manchester Center, VT), Cornell Campus Store Warehouse (Ithaca, NY), Little Professor (Northington, OH), Joseph-Beth Booksellers (Lexington, KY), Davis-Kidd Booksellers (Nashville, TN), Library Limited (Clayton, MO), Varney's Bookstore (Manhattan, KS), McKinzey-White Booksellers (Colorado Springs, CO), Ex Libris Bookstore (Sun Valley, ID), and Bookshop Santa Cruz (Santa Cruz, CA).

For whatever reasons, he had never spoken in his own backyard, so when word got out that he'd be hosting one of his "Evenings" at the Bangor Auditorium, the event was an instant sell-out. Because it was open seating, the lines started forming in late afternoon for the show.

The doors opened and the crowd poured into the auditorium, surprised to find signed copies of *Rose Madder* for sale. Although

King answers a question during his 1997 "Evening" at Bangor Auditorium.

The logo for King's coast-to-coast motorcyle tour to promote *Insomnia*.

limited to one per customer, the stock sold out long before the evening ended.

Over the years, King has standardized his "Evening" shows: after an introduction, he usually warms up the crowd by chatting for a half hour, bringing them up-to-date on whatever's on his mind, followed by a reading—typically from a forthcoming book—and caps it off with a question-and-answer session, which can run on (if the questions are thought-provoking) or be cut off after fifteen minutes if he deems the questions inane.

As usual, King spoke without notes or props of any kind, and the audience hung on every word, eager to hear anything he had to say. King, in short, had his usual captive audience.

After Tabitha King introduced herself and dead-panned that her husband also wrote—predictably, it got a lot of laughs—Stephen King took to the stage to thunderous applause and talked about the inspiration for *Desperation*, followed by a riveting reading from its first chapter.

Afterward, King took questions from the audience, but after fifteen minutes of maddening questions from tongue-tied fans, King cited "fanny fatigue" and called it a night, leaving the stage to thunderous applause.

Above: A guitar signed by all members of the Rock Bottom Remainders
is raffled off to raise money for a local charity.
Right: A poster announcing the first-ever Rock Bottom Remainders concert.

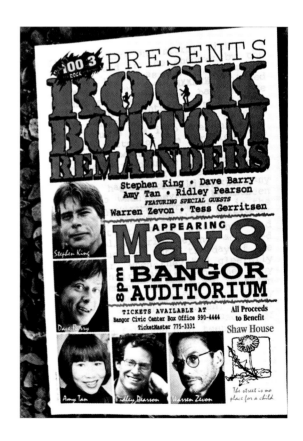

The boogeyman belts out a solo.

The Rock Bottom Remainders

> We're extremely excited about finally playing right here in River City. This will be a fun show for a very good cause.
>
> —Stephen King, *The Shaw House Quarterly* (May 1988)

Four years after his "Evening with Stephen King," Bangor's favorite boogeyman again took to the stage at the Bangor Auditorium—to rock, not to read. King orchestrated a rare appearance of the Rock Bottom Remainders, sponsored by King's rock-and-roll radio station, WKIT.

The Remainders' first concert was in May 1992 at the Cowboy Boogie in Anaheim, California, in front of a capacity crowd composed of convention attendees from the American Booksellers Convention. It was intended to be a one-shot event, but the members were having so much fun—hey, any excuse not to write—that they rocked on, raising money for numerous charities.

They hit the road like any other band, traveling down the east coast from New England to Florida, an adventure chronicled in *Mid-life Confidential*, a book King suggested to finance the road tour, with contributions from all the band members and snapshots by Tabitha King. (Ironically, the book was latered remaindered at a rock-bottom price.)

For their first-ever appearance in Bangor, King arranged a few surprises: Maine governor Angus King appeared—wearing sunglasses, clad in a black leather jacket and jeans, on a Harley (he and King are both Harley men)—as the band struck up "Leader of the Pack;" Joel Selvin literally screamed for a half minute at the top of his lungs, while performing an X-rated version of "Louie, Louie;" a leather-clad Amy Tan belted out the Nancy Sinatra song, "These Boots Are Made for Walking," and playfully mock-brandished a leather whip in the direction of the band members' proffered bottoms; and Dave Barry and his wife shared a duet, "Love Is Strange."

But King fans were there to see not Angus but Stephen, who broke out in a wide smile when rocker Warren Zevon played the guitar behind his back.

And if all that weren't enough, King—Stephen, not Angus—howled like a werewolf as he belted out Zevon's most famous song, "Werewolves of London."

A titanic show, in my opinion, and a night to remember.

Christopher Spruce, the General Manager of WKIT, which sponsored the event, was correct when he said beforehand, "Guaranteed that this will be a show to remember. This may be the one and only time the Remainders play in Bangor."

If so, too bad; the Rock Bottom Remainders are one hell of a band.

Left: Warren Zevon and Stephen King jam on guitar. Right: Dave Barry, humorist and author, treats the audience to "Gloria."

The monsters turned out in droves, as did the media, because it was the world premiere of *Stephen King's Graveyard Shift*. The premiere was held not in Hollywood, but in Bangor at the Hoyt's Cinema, on October 25, 1990. Predictably, King was the big draw, especially since he was instrumental in forcing Hollywood to film in Maine a feature-length adaptation of his short story, "Graveyard Shift."

The lobby was decorated thematically with banners from the movie, a coffin bearing the legend "Stephen King's Graveyard Shift," with refreshments set up for the media, including a giant cake meticulously formed in the shape of a giant rat. (I thought the coconut was a nice touch, giving the "ratcake" an appropriately furry look.) Outside, long lines of local kids showed up in costumes, from vampires to monsters, eager to gain free admission to the premiere.

King arrived and took his place at the table set up for him. He was joined by the film's screenwriter John Esposito and the film's co-producer, a fellow Mainer, William Dunn.

Local ghouls dress up to get free tickets to the premiere of *Graveyard Shift* at Hoyt's Cinema in Bangor in 1990.

By filming entirely in Maine, *Graveyard Shift* pumped an estimated $3 million into Bangor, Lewiston, and Lisbon Center. Budgeted at $10.5 million, the film had an unmistakably gritty look and feel to it, showing a side of Maine that most tourists never see—the long-abandoned mills in small-town Maine, once a symbol of industrial strength but now just abandoned relics as its jobs went out of state, usually overseas.

A gruesome story that originally appeared in *Cavalier* (October 1970), "Graveyard Shift" is the story of Hall, a drifter who works at a mill in Gates Fall, Maine. He prefers working the late-night hours from 11 P.M. to 7 A.M., when it's coolest.

During a holiday, Hall and others volunteer to clean out the mill's basement. To their surprise, they find a subcellar. Opening that, they find a world of strange, mutated rats, including winged ones and an eyeless, legless rat "as big as a Holstein calf," among other monstrosities.

In other words, it's Stephen King country, with terror, horror, and gross-out galore—the three dictums of the horror tale, as he notes in *Danse Macabre*: "I recognize terror as the finest emotion and so I will try to terrorize the reader. But if I find that I cannot terrify, I will try to horrify, and if I find that I can't horrify, I'll go for the gross-out."

At the *Graveyard Shift* press conference, King said:

"Graveyard Shift" was written by this 22-year-old kid who sold two pieces of fiction beforehand, to specialty magazines. That kid was still in school when the story was written and rewritten. It's a very early piece of work. It is in fact the second earliest piece of fiction I've ever included in any of my published works.

It was put together years later by people who are seasoned, people who have worked in this field a long time, in any number of capacities.

In a way, John Esposito and I are the perfect team, in terms of him adapting my material, because we were both starting out, cutting our teeth. And you have advantages that balance off the disadvantages of being new—boundless enthusiasm, which John has, and the ability to go for it all, which is automatic when you're starting out.

Whether or not *Graveyard Shift* does its job in terms of art, I don't much care. It works in terms of sitting back and putting your feet up and watching the movie and having a good time. We'll let Martin Scorsese and those guys take care of themselves; they didn't make this movie—this movie was made by cannibals.

The movie, however, was not consumed by the critics with relish. Most felt it was a one-note story, an insufficient vehicle for a full-length motion picture. The *Washington Post* summed up the feelings of many others who damned the film, noting that "The acting and directing are substandard. Even the hackneyed plot is barely turned over. . . . Even the jaws of life couldn't extricate this film from the quick burial it deserves."

Some years later, the Hoyt's Cinema itself served as the inspiration for an original King screenplay, *Stephen King's Sleepwalkers*.

King's oldest son, then seventeen, had a crush on the popcorn girl at the cinema. King told interviewer W. C. Stroby:

At the premiere of *Graveyard Shift*, King makes a point while co-producer Bill Dunn and screenwriter Joe Esposito look on.

So we listened to a lot of agonizing at my house about Joe's crush on this popcorn girl, and one night when we were at the movies, he was talking to her and I saw why he was attracted to her. She was just this beautiful, vital girl who played a lot of sports and had this kind of healthy, wholesome glow about her. . . . And it made me think of a guy wanting to ask the popcorn girl out for all the wrong reasons, and the story just sort of followed that burst of inspiration.

The story that resulted, King's first original film script, focused on Charles Brady, a handsome young boy with a crush on the popcorn girl at the local cinema. He is on the prowl for young, virginal girls . . . but not for himself: He wants them for his mother who, like him, is a Sleepwalker, an immortal who must feed on the life forces of young girls in order to rejuvenate herself.

King's final assessment on the flick: "I'd probably give it a B plus," he told *Fangoria* magazine.

THE BANGOR INTERNATIONAL AIRPORT

If you fly into the Bangor International Airport—one of two modern jetports in the state—don't be surprised if you experience déjà vu. Chances are you've seen it before, in *Pet Sematary* or, more likely, in the ABC-TV miniseries *The Langoliers*.

In 1988 the terminal was transformed to accommodate shooting for *Pet Sematary*. Both United and Eastern Express Airlines donated planes for the shoot; Delta Airlines donated two gates; and the airport itself saw up to ninety extras on its set.

The only difference between this Cessna and the one the vampire flew in King's "The Night Flier" is the number on the tail.

Part of the terminal was transformed to resemble Boston's Logan Airport. It was so convincing, said the *Bangor Daily News*, that "a large sign welcoming passengers to Boston had to be covered up during the day in order not to confuse real-life travelers."

In 1994, the ABC-TV miniseries, *The Langoliers*—based on King's novella—was filmed at BIA. It tells of a red-eye flight originally headed to Boston's Logan Airport which passes through a twilight zone to emerge in a curiously altered world in which the Langoliers are literally erasing the landscape, a world from which they must escape by going back through the twilight zone—a rip in time, as it were—to the world as they know it.

"The Night Flier"

Near the main terminal at BIA, a smaller terminal houses the private planes, mostly single- and double-prop planes, workhorses like the Cessna, which King termed the Chevy of small planes.

It's the same kind of plane that was used by a vampire in King's "The Night Flier." This vampire broke with tradition and, instead of turning into a bat to fly, he flew the unfriendly skies in his Skymaster, a Cessna 337, bearing the tail number N101BL.

The vampire, a night flier, haunts small airports where he knows he can feed undisturbed, until Richard Dees, a reporter from a tabloid newspaper, catches his scent and takes off in hot pursuit.

You've seen the places where the Kings have lived, but do you know of their philanthropy? It's the least publicized aspect of their lives and, arguably, the most significant.

Stephen King's trek from a life of genteel poverty in Durham to unimaginable fame and riches in Bangor has given him a unique perspective: he knows how tough life can be for the less fortunate, so when he can afford to spend time, money, and energy to improve the quality of life in Bangor and the surrounding towns, he and his wife do so gladly, investing millions of dollars through their foundation.

You may recognize the interior of the Bangor International Airport from *The Langoliers,* an ABC miniseries that was filmed here.

No UMaine graduate has "made it" on the scale that Stephen King has made it. Yet he and Tabitha chose to stay and raise their kids in Bangor, Maine. Their generosity in the community is legendary and Maine is a much better place because they are here.

—*Maine* (winter/spring 1997 issue)

CHAPTER 3: CHARITY BEGINS AT HOME—
THE KINGS' PHILANTHROPY

Shakespeare was wrong: the good that men do is not always interred with their bags of bones.

In Stephen and Tabitha King's case, their roots in Maine and especially in the local community run deep; they want to give back and make a difference, and they surely have.

Understandably, like most people who can afford to give magnanimously of their money and their time, they'd prefer to keep their generosity low-profile, since the more exposure they get, the more it draws requests; still, the press—especially in Maine—has publicized the Kings' philanthropy on TV, radio, and in print, making it clear that the most famous residents of the state are also among the most generous with their assets.

No one—outside of those involved in administering the Stephen and Tabitha King Foundation, which tithes ten percent of King's income to charities—knows exactly the dispensation of their donations, since some were given with specific instructions to keep a low profile.

For instance, on the Kings' sizable donation to the Bangor YMCA, director Chris Mogridge demurred discussing it, saying, "The Kings have made it very clear that

Above: William Cohen, chairman of the Bangor City Council, gives Stephen and Tabitha the key to the city at the dedication of the Shawn Trevor Mansfield Baseball Complex, June 1, 1992. (Photo courtesy of the *Bangor Daily News*)

Stephen King and Tabitha recieve the Norbert K. Dowd Highest Achievement Award for contributing to the social and economic well-being of the Bangor area, January, 1992. (Photo courtesy of the *Bangor Daily News*)

they want this kept as quiet as possible."

Toward fund-raising vehicles, the Kings typically donate twenty-five to thirty-five percent to get the ball rolling, requesting that the city match it and that the local community make up the difference. An equitable arrangement, it gives everyone an incentive to dig in deep and contribute.

Some of the Kings' more publicized donations include:

·$2.5 million in matching funds for the Bangor Public Library.

·$1.2 million for the Shawn Trevor Mansfield Baseball Complex in Hayford Park.

·$4 million to the University of Maine, with an initial donation of $1 million and annual donations for the next three years of $1 million, contingent on the effective use of the money.

·$750,000 to the Eastern Maine Medical Center, for funding toward a pediatrics ward.

·$750,000 toward a 6,000 square-foot addition to the Old Town public library, named the Tabitha Jane Spruce King Wing in her honor.

·A standing offer to match any donation of $1,000 or more—up to $40,000—to the United Way of Penobscot Valley.

·An undisclosed amount to the varsity swim team at UMO. (King's comment to the hometown newspaper: "I wanted to preserve my right to say two things. There's something wrong with a system where the hockey team can go to Los Angeles and the swimming team can't go to Bridgeport, Conn. I think they did go, but there was talk they wouldn't. The other thing I wanted to say is that the University of Maine has got to be able to do something for these kids. There's got to be a continuing effort to look around and help these programs that don't get on TV.")

·$50,000 to the Mount Desert Island swim team.

·$150,000 to the YMCA at Orono, with the challenge issued for anyone to match his donation.

·An undisclosed amount to the Bangor YMCA, which Stephen King frequents.

·$40,000 for recovering alcoholics (organization not specified).

·$29,000 to the Pine Tree Chapter of the American Red Cross.

·$10,000 to the Dana-Farber Cancer Institute.

·$5,000 to the United Negro College Fund.

·$40,000 to the National Poetry Foundation at UMO.

·$30,000 to the Shaw House in Bangor. (King also arranged for a Rock Bottom Remainders concert in May 1998 to raise money for this shelter for teenagers.)

The Kings contributed to the funding of the KIDS Bangor Creative Playground.

The KIDS playground was built over the course of one week in the fall of 1988.

·An undisclosed donation toward the $12.5 million needed to build an arts and music center at Milton Academy in Milton, Massachusetts. (The Ruth King Theater, which opened in 1991, was named after Stephen King's mother, who was a talented piano player and organist. Said Stephen King: "As children, we need to have our dreams encouraged and nurtured. My mother did that for me.")

·A blank check from Tabitha King for KIDS: Bangor Creative Playground, built during September 28 to October 9, 1998, and adjacent to the Shawn Trevor Mansfield Baseball Complex.

·Undisclosed sums over the years for individual scholarships at Hampden Academy and for many other causes.

In January 1992, the Kings were presented the Norbert K. Dowd Award for service to the community at the annual dinner of the Greater Bangor Chamber of Commerce, at which attendees paid thirty dollars a head. At the event, Maine humorist Tim Sample said, "In a decade when selfishness was an icon, the 1980s, Stephen and Tabitha made generosity a hallmark."

In accepting the award, King said that in 1979 they "looked to settle for good" and narrowed the choice between Portland and Bangor, but they chose the latter because it had a "sense of community with no frills." King added that they never had second thoughts after taking Bangor to their hearts. "We've never said, 'Maybe life would have been better if we had gone to the southern part of the state.' We're glad to be part of Bangor. Whatever we've done for Bangor was the result of what Bangor has done for us."

Bangor, clearly, had taken the Kings to its heart, as well.

> There's no Bahamian retreat, no yacht, no plane. I don't own my money,
> I'm a custodian. How do I do the best with it?
>
> —Stephen King, in "King of Bangor" by James Conaway

The state's most famous native-born author, Stephen King, makes millions out of horror stories straight from an unconscious that seems tied to some sublime gothic quality in the Maine air and landscape.

—Neil Rolde, *Maine: A Narrative History*

PART 2
KING'S LITERARY MAP

CHAPTER 4: FICTIONAL MAINE HAUNTS

Stephen King calls them his "peculiar places," which is an apt description. The sole cartographer of his imaginary landscape, King is your only reliable guide to these eerie locales, which can't be found on any map; he's also your only hope in getting back.

Frankly, I don't know why you'd want to visit these towns, because most people who do either barely escape with their lives or never make it out alive.

King's fictional world is populated with these offbeat locations. Though each is different, whether set in Maine or out of state, all share a common theme: the landscape is surreal, shifting from the real world to an unreal world, where everything that's familiar becomes increasingly unfamiliar, as if the landscape is literally metamorphosing.

Early in his career, when Stephen King contemplated writing a vampire novel, he had initial misgivings about its small-town setting, Jerusalem's Lot. The FBI, he told his wife and Chris Chesley, equipped with the most modern crime-fighting equipment would quickly track down and capture any elusive miscreant, human or supernatural. But, as Tabitha and Chris pointed out, they'd have to find them first. As they reminded Stephen, there were parts of Maine where you could get lost and never be found, and certainly not if you didn't want to be found.

King agreed and his vampire novel *'Salem's Lot* (1975)—a contraction for Jerusalem's Lot—was set in small-town Maine, not unlike the places where King had spent most of his early years.

Above: This view of the Androscroggin River in Lisbon Falls could easily be the setting for a scene in one of King's novels.

Folks in Maine give Jerusalem's Lot—they call it 'Salem's Lot—a wide berth, especially at night. In *'Salem's Lot*, John Lewis, a features editor for the *Press Herald*, publishes an article "Ghost Town in Maine?" in which he notes that it is "a small town east of Cumberland and twenty miles north of Portland. It is not the first town in American history to just dry up and blow away, and will probably not be the last, but it is one of the strangest." For its 1970 census, Lewis notes, the town counted 1,319 people, which included "exactly 67 souls in the ten years since the previous census."

These sixty-seven townsfolk dropped out of sight, according to Lewis. They simply picked up stakes and left, most refusing to talk about why they left.

But the rumors flew. "'Salem's Lot is reputed to be haunted," wrote Lewis. Something happened and 'Salem's Lot is now a ghost town. Lewis wrote, "There are no children; only abandoned shops and stores, deserted houses, overgrown lawns, deserted streets, and back roads."

The town, King tells us, is laid out in four quadrants. North Jerusalem comprises the mostly wooded high ground, which is where the Marsten House is sited. The northeast is mostly open land, through which runs the Royal River, feeding into the Androscoggin. The southeast "was the prettiest," with farms and houses owned by white-collar workers. (The Griffen's barn was the major landmark in this sector.) But the southwest quadrant has gone to seed, with unkempt trailers and run-down houses that King terms "kissing cousins to woodsheds."

It's September 5, 1975, and Ben Mears, a writer who grew up in 'Salem's Lot twenty-five years ago, has returned to write a novel, using the town as his inspiration. He thinks of renting the Marsten House—so named for its owner, Hubert Marsten, who booby-trapped the house, then hung himself from a bedroom rafter—but instead, rents a place at Eva's Rooms, a boarding house, where he takes a room on the third floor, which is almost unbearably hot because it's summer and the room is not air-conditioned.

The Marsten House is purchased by an outsider, a bald man who, even in the summer heat, doesn't sweat. An odd-looking man who speaks in a flat tone of voice, Richard Throckett Straker pays a visit to Crockett's Southern Maine Insurance and Realty, where he surprises its proprietor, Lawrence Crockett, by offering one dollar for the Marsten House.

Incredulous, Crockett listens to Straker's offer and, to his surprise, realizes that the stranger has come prepared with all the papers in order and an offer too good to be true: In exchange for handling the transaction and keeping quiet, Crockett will get the land on which a future shopping mall will be built. "He had overthrown his own personal maxim for the first time: You don't shit where you eat," King wrote.

Straker, a familiar for something more sinister, has come to town, but to most people he is not what he appears to be: an odd outsider who will lose his shirt opening up an antique store. What the locals don't see is that the antique store is merely a front for Straker's master, Kurt Barlow, who comes from the old world, a very old world, where immortals walked—no, *haunted*—the earth, in search of prey.

Barlow, a vampire, is about to slake his immortal thirst on the hapless townspeople of Jerusalem's Lot, who will become Un-Dead, serving the new, dark master until Ben Mears, aided by Father Callahan and Mark Petrie, puts an end to Barlow's unholy reign of terror.

As the novel ends, Mears deliberately lights a Pall Mall cigarette and throws it into the brush; and the wind, blowing from the west, pushes the fire toward town, toward the vampires who will soon be on the run.

But sometimes they come back.

In King's short story, "One for the Road," found in *Night Shift*—his first short fiction collection—it's January, and a storm has blanketed southern Maine with six inches of snow and more on the way. Herb "Tookey" Tooklander, of Tookey's Bar, tells Booth, the narrator, to have one for the road before he shuts down. There are no customers, after all, and the weather isn't getting any better. But just then, a stranger staggers in and faints.

When he comes to, they hear his story.

His name is Gerard Lumley, and he's come for help. He drove off the road after taking a bad turn near 'Salem's Lot, where he left his wife and daughter in the car. He walked six miles for help, ending up at Tookey's, more out of luck than intent.

When Lumley mentions the Lot, and how odd it was that there were no lights on in the town, Booth, the story's narrator, recalls that a few years ago, folks there started disappearing, and those foolish enough to move in soon moved out. "Then the town burned flat. It was at end of a long dry fall. They figured it started up by the Marsten House. . . . It burned out of control for three days."

The three of them climb into Tookey's Scout—a four-wheel drive vehicle that can negotiate the hellish storm—and head back toward the place where Lumley abandoned his car, leaving his wife and child to whatever might come to them in the storm— creatures of the night, vampires that somehow survived the great conflagration.

When Lumley sees his wife, he runs to her, but quickly draws back when he gets near, because he sees that she's undead. It's too late, and she attacks and kills her mortal husband.

Lumley, though, is not the only one who gets a vampiric visitation. Lumley's angelic little girl Francie, aged seven, wants to give Booth "a little kiss," a vampire's kiss.

The Shiloh Church in Durham is rumored to be the inspiration for the Marsten House in *'Salem's Lot*.

Francie "was going to be seven for an eternity of nights. Her little face was a ghastly corpse white, her eyes a red and silver that you could fall into. And below her jaw I could see two small punctures like pinpricks," Barton observed.

Barton and Tookey escape, but over the years others fall victim, as King explains: "a hitchhiker will disappear around there someplace, up on Schoolyard Hill or out near the Harmony Hill Cemetery." So if you're at Tookey's Bar, cautions Barton, ". . . have your drink, and then my advice to you is to keep right on moving north. Whatever you do, don't go up that road to Jerusalem's Lot. Especially not after dark."

There are towns in Maine that are havens, but this town isn't one of them. In *The Tommyknockers*, published by Putnam in 1987, King takes us to what used to be a quiet, small Maine town, until the Tommyknockers came knocking.

Life in Haven takes a turn for the worse when, on June 21, 1988, Roberta "Bobbie" Anderson, accompanied by her dog Pete, heads down an old logging road, looking for wood to cut, to lay in a supply for the winter. Then she trips over three inches of dull metal protruding out of the ground. She touches the metal and it vibrates. Odd.

Optimistic, she begins digging, thinking she can excavate it, but she's wrong. That night, when she falls asleep, she has a strange dream in which all of her teeth, one by one, fall out . . . and she sees a strange green light. Very odd.

Bobbie doesn't know it, but buried deep in the ground, where it has stayed for millennia, is a large starship inhabited by the Tommyknockers, "interstellar gypsies with no king," as Stephen King put it.

The Tommyknockers, however, are now alive and begin to exert their otherworldly influence on the Havenites, beginning with Bobbie, a novelist. When Jim Gardener visits Bobbie, he's surprised to find that her hot water heater, which used to run on LP gas, now runs by itself, jury-rigged with what appears to be a self-contained force field. (That's one house the local natural gas company, Dead River Gas of Derry, won't need to visit anytime soon.) Likewise, when he sees her tractor, a modified Tomcat with an "UP" setting for vertical rise, Gardener knows something is very wrong indeed. The final proof: He is amazed to discover that she has somehow written a 400-page novel, *The Buffalo Soldiers*, in three weeks, "a novel that was, just incidentally, the best thing she had ever written."

Not only are the gadgets and the novel disquieting, but when Gardener sees Bobbie, she looks emaciated; just as inexplicable, her teeth are falling out. Bobbie's body is literally wasting away, for which no earthly explanation is possible. (Of course, there's a very good unearthly explanation—the Tommyknockers' evil influence.)

Rather than try to explain her mysterious contraptions, Bobbie gives a demonstration. Gardner rolls some paper into her modified typewriter and, as she thinks the words, the typewriter starts clattering away. That is the explanation for how the novel was written so quickly, an explanation that Gardener would not have believed unless he had seen it himself.

"This isn't really a typewriter at all anymore. It's a dream machine. One that dreams rationally. There's something cosmically funny about them giving it to me, so I could write *The Buffalo Soldiers*," she explains.

Cosmic, yes, but funny? No.

Bobbie Anderson is not the only one affected in Haven.

Hilly Brown, a young boy whose mind is bursting with great, new ideas for magic tricks, puts on his Second Gala Magic Show, aided by his younger brother David, who is billed as "the Disappearing Human!"

In front of an uncomprehending audience, Hilly makes his brother disappear—a trick he learned from the Tommyknockers—but they haven't told him how to bring his brother back, nor does Hilly have any earthly idea himself.

His brother, though, isn't going to come back. Hilly has a mental image of his brother suffocating to death under alien skies "maybe a trillion miles from home." And so it went. In a peculiar inversion of the common admonition from 1950s science-fiction movies, the danger faced by the Havenites came not from the skies but from the ground.

A portion of the Barrens, a prominent landmark in *IT*.

When Stephen King moved to Bangor to buy a house and decided to make it his winter home—his summer home at Center Lovell would be his haven away from the pressing crowds—he knew Bangor was rich with story possibilities; there was, as King said in *Black Magic & Music: A Novelist's Perspective on Bangor* (1983), unmined lore in the Queen city. Here King wrote about his fascination with Bangor and his desire to set a long novel in the city. The novel, he wrote, is titled *Derry*.

The 1,138-page novel was published, but the working title of *Derry* was discarded in favor of *IT* (1986), a reference to the creature that lives in a sewer, a shape-shifting monster who haunts a band of Derry youths who, years later as adults, band together again to confront, and ultimately defeat, IT. A complex story on two parallel timestreams—1957 and 1985—*IT* is, as the *Los Angeles Herald Examiner* put it, "Epic . . . gargantuan . . . breathlessly accelerating suspense . . . the *Moby Dick* of horror novels."

Equipped with a street map of Bangor, you would be able to identify on a walking or driving tour much of the geography found in *IT*. In addition, the references to Bangor and the greater Bangor area dot the novel's imaginative landscape. Let me give you just a taste of what to expect, of the real-world/fictional world linkages:

• The Barrens: "[A] messy track of land about a mile and a half wide by three miles long. It was bounded by upper Kansas Street on one side and by old Cape on the

Above: The Derry Library, which plays a significant role in *IT*, is modeled on the Bangor Public Library on Harlow Street.
Below: To date, King's books have been translated into more than 30 languages and have sold more than 50 million copies overseas. The French edition of *IT* is called *ÇA*.
Opposite: The Standpipe, a prominent landmark in Bangor and Derry.

other." (In the novel, this is where the sewer pipes lead underground, to IT's lair.) Running diagonally through Bangor, northwest to southeast, this place can be found flanking Valley Avenue, north of exit 47 off the Interstate.

·Bassey Park: In *IT*, this is the park that flanks the high school. Real-life Bangor has a Bass Park.

·The Derry Library: For two of the Losers—Ben Hanscomb and Mike Hanlon—this library was especially significant: It was Ben's favorite place as a child; and as an adult, it was Hanlon's place of employment. (He also kept in its vault his manuscript, "Derry: An Unauthorized Town History.") Real-life Bangor's Public Library is situated on Harlow Street.

·The Derry Mall: In *IT*, Dave Gardener had one of his Shoeboat retail stores in this mall. Bangor has Bangor Mall, now the major shopping area of the city.

·The Frati Brothers Pawnshop: In the novel, this store was replaced in 1985 by a Trustworthy Hardware Store. In Bangor, not far from Betts Bookstore, you'll find the Frati Brothers Pawnshop.

·Mount Hope Cemetery: In *IT*, this was where George Denbrough was buried. (Readers of *Pet Sematary* will probably notice that this was where Gage Creed was buried.) In Bangor, the Mount Hope Cemetery is where, for the film version of *Pet Sematary*,

Stephen King, as a minister, presided over Creed's funeral at this real-life cemetery in Bangor.

• Penobscot County: Fictional Derry as well as real-life Bangor are located in this county.

• Penobscot River: The sewers in Derry empty into the Penobscot; running east-west, it bisects Bangor and Brewer.

• St. Joseph's Hospital: After she broke her leg in a car crash, Cheryl Tarrent was taken here. In reality, located in Bangor.

The Standpipe at night.

• Shawshank (fictional): A Maine prison where an Air Force colonel is sent after getting Cheryl Lamonica pregnant. (This is also where Andy Dufresne was incarcerated, in "Rita Hayworth and Shawshank Redemption.")

• The Standpipe: A prominent landmark in Derry, a water tower that holds almost two million gallons. Real-life Bangor's Standpipe, on top of a hill, is one of its most prominent landmarks, towering over the city.

• The University of Maine: Two of the Losers—Bill Denbrough and Mike Hanlon—graduated from here. . . . Stephen and Tabitha King—and Stephen's childhood friend Chris Chesley—are graduates of this university.

• The Viking Press: The publishing house in New York City where Bill Denbrough submitted his first novel, a horror story about ghosts. Before King defected to Scribner, he was published in hardcover by Viking.

• West Broadway: The street in Derry known for its mansions and Bangor's most famous street historically, where the lumber barons at the turn of the century made their homes. The Kings' home is on West Broadway.

In reading King, the sense you get is that his literary landscape—a geographic jigsaw puzzle—is an ongoing exploration, for not only was *IT* set in the mythical Derry, but so is *Insomnia* and, most recently, *Bag of Bones*.

*You couldn't have picked a better day
to come back to Castle Rock.*

—narrator's introduction to *Needful Things*

CASTLE ROCK

Above: Runaround Pond, where Jimmy Smith of *The Dead Zone* has a skating accident, is also where a young King used to play with his childhood friend Chris Chesley.

For King fans, Castle Rock is the main terrain, the place the author has visited so often that he knows where all the roads go. Taking its name from a place in William Golding's *The Lord of the Flies*, Castle Rock provides the setting for *The Dead Zone*, *Cujo*, "The Body," *The Dark Half*, "The Sun Dog," and *Needful Things*. It is also the name of the film company at which former TV star/director Rob Reiner produced *Misery*, *Stand by Me*, and *Needful Things*.

The Dead Zone

A monster has come to Castle Rock. The monster, though, is not a supernatural boogeyman but is, in fact, a human monster, dubbed the Castle Rock Killer. After John Chancellor of *NBC News* reports that five women in as many years have been raped and strangled by the elusive Castle Rock Killer, he reports that a nine-year-old girl has just become his sixth victim.

The network then picks up the local feed from the on-location reporter, Catherine Mackin, who states quietly, "A sense of quietly mounting hysteria lies over this small New England mill town this afternoon. The townspeople of Castle Rock have been nervous for a long time over the unknown person the local press calls 'the Castle Rock Strangler' or sometimes 'the November Killer.' That nervousness has changed to terror—no one here thinks that word is too strong—following the discovery of Mary Kate Hendrasen's body on the town common."

One viewer, Johnny Smith, picks up the phone and wants to talk to Sheriff Bannerman in Castle Rock. Smith knows the identity of the killer who is no stranger to Sheriff Bannerman himself.

It all begins in January 1953 when Johnny Smith (of Pownal, Maine) is skating backward on Runaround Pond in nearby Durham. Another kid, playing hockey, rams into him and knocks him down. Johnny Smith blacks out.

After that accident, however, Johnny has "hunches—he would know what the next record on the radio was going to be before the DJ played it, that sort of thing—but he never connected these with his accident on the ice. By then he had forgotten it."

Smith's wheel of misfortune continues and years later, as an adult, the wheel spins again. This time, Smith's car, out of commission, is being worked on at Tibbets Garage in Hampden. A teacher at Cleave Mills High, Smith is dating a fellow teacher, Sarah Bracknell.

Cleave Mills, we are told, is such a small town that it consists of "mostly a main street with a stop-and-go light at the Intersection (it turned into a blinker after 6 P.M.), about two dozen stores, and a small moccasin factory." (It is near Orono.)

Johnny and Sarah are on a date in nearby Esty, about twenty miles north of Orono, at its annual agricultural fair. While there, Smith wins $540 at the Wheel of Fortune, which prompts the carny to shut down the game. As the two leave and head back to her house, Johnny Smith's fortune takes another turn—this time for the worse—when he elects to take a cab home.

But Johnny never makes it home. A pair of cars racing in the night, are heading toward the cab, and the cabbie—distracted by his conversation about Nixon and the Vietnam War—turns too late, seeing the oncoming pairs of headlights bearing down on him.

Johnny Smith is taken to the Eastern Maine Medical Center and, remains there almost five years. After reemerging he's psychic; he sees into what he calls the dead zone, which is how he knows the identity of the rapist and strangler that's haunting Castle Rock.

The human monster is Frank Dodd, a twenty-five-year-old man who lives with his mother. He is characterized by a disbelieving Sheriff Bannerman as "a fine officer and a fine man. He's crossing over next November to run for municipal chief of police, and he'll do it with my blessing. . . . Johnny, you put your foot in the bucket. Frank Dodd is no murderer. I'd stake my life on that."

But it's the damned truth. Dodd is the murderer, and when Johnny Smith and Sheriff Bannerman go to Dodd's mother's home, they find him in the bathroom, naked save for a black raincoat, with a self-inflicted fatal wound. King tells us, "Around Frank Dodd's neck on a string was a sign crayoned in lipstick. It read: I CONFESS."

Cujo

In *Cujo*, published by Viking in 1981, Frank Dodd sets the stage for a story about a rabid 200-pound, Saint Bernard dog that belongs to Joe Camber, who runs a garage on the outskirts of Castle Rock. "He was not werewolf, vampire, ghoul, or unnamable creature from the enchanted forest or from the snowy wastes; he was only a cop named Frank Dodd with mental and sexual problems. . . . A town's nightmares were buried in Frank Dodd's grave," King writes.

Invoked by the elders when they wanted to keep their kids in line, Dodd has been dead in his grave for five years, but as King wrote, "The monster never dies. . . . It came to Castle Rock again in the summer of 1980." It comes in the form of *Cujo*, Joe Camber's friendly dog that turns rabid after being bitten on the nose by a bat. *Cujo* is another chapter in the history of this small Maine town that King knows all too well.

"The Body"

Dedicated to George McLeod, who gave him the germ of the idea (McLeod told him about a dead dog that he had seen on the railroad tracks), this story is King's most autobiographical and, as a result, it hits hard, a centerpunch to the heart.

Most people who know this story came to know it not because of its print publication in *Different Seasons* but because of Castle Rock's masterful film adaptation, *Stand By Me*. King and Reiner saw the film together at a public theater; afterward, Reiner, quoted in *Stephen King: At the Movies*, said he could see that King was visibly moved.

The story revolves around the late Ray Brower, a boy killed in a railroad accident, according to a news broadcast the boys heard on WLAM radio, broadcasting out of Lewiston. Brower, King writes, "was from Chamberlain, a town forty miles or so east of

Opposite: The four boys in *Stand By Me* walk along a railroad trestle track similar to this one in Lisbon Falls.

110   KING'S LITERARY MAP

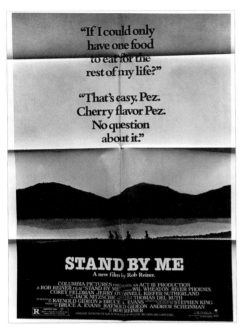

The movie *Stand By Me* (1986) was based on King's novella, "The Body."

Castle Rock." (Chamberlain, located east of Boothbay Harbor, is on the coastline. On the real-world map, Castle Rock would be out in the Atlantic Ocean.)

The "surrounding towns" near Chamberlain, King writes, are "Motton, Durham and Pownal," the latter two of which are located near Lisbon Falls. (Note: Motton is the locale for the award-winning story, "The Man in the Black Suit.")

In "The Body," four boys—including the narrator Gordon "Gordie" Lachance—take a trek to see Brower's body and, in doing so, make a journey toward adulthood, from innocence to experience.

After the boys encounter leeches in a pond hugging close to shore—one drawn from King's teen experiences with leeches at Runaround Pond in Durham—the four boys have to travel, by foot, sixteen miles to reach Back Harlow Road, near Royal River (on a real-world map, it is west of Pownal and Durham, with train tracks running parallel to it).

The four finally find Brower's body, but it is anticlimactic. To use an appropriate cliché, it was the journey, not the destination, that was important.

The Castle Rock Trilogy

> William Faulkner's imaginative, intuitive cosmos—Yoknapatawpha County —was one of the most convincing ever conceived by a writer. His own "little postage stamp of native soil," as he called it, was a spiritual kingdom that he transmuted into a microcosm not only of the South but also of the human race.
>
> —Willie Morris, "Faulkner's Mississippi," in *National Geographic*, March 1989 issue

In a note that precedes "The Sun Dog" (in *Four Past Midnight*), King explains that *The Dark Half* (1989), "The Sun Dog" (1990), and *Needful Things* (1991) comprise "a Castle Rock Trilogy, if you please—the last Castle Rock stories."

The Dark Half

The Dark Half is a novel about Thad Beaumont and George Stark—the former's dark half, his murderous pen name that comes to life to haunt him. Thad and Liz Beaumont have a summer home in Castle Rock, where Sheriff Alan Pangborn pays them a visit to investigate a brutal murder.

"The Sun Dog" (in *Four Past Midnight*)

Pangborn reappears in "The Sun Dog," a novella set in Castle Rock that serves as a narrative bridge, setting the stage for the final Castle Rock story, *Needful Things*.

In "The Sun Dog," Kevin Delevan gets a birthday gift that appears to be an ordinary Sun Polaroid camera, but it's nothing of the sort. In fact, as Kevin shoots photos, it records the most curious pictures: a beastly-looking dog bounds, with each snapshot, toward the photographer, looking to attack. (What, one wonders, happens when the dog has in fact bounded out of the picture frame?)

In "The Sun Dog," we see old characters reappear, and new ones introduced, as well. In addition to Big George Bannerman (the Castle Rock sheriff killed by Cujo), Joe Camber is mentioned—he was Cujo's owner in *Cujo*. And that no-account Ace Merrill ("The Body") breaks into the Mellow Tiger, his favorite bar. He is sent up the river to Shawshank Prison for a four-year term, but as usual has mischief on his mind. (His arresting officer is Sheriff Pangborn.)

We meet, for the first time, Polly Chalmers, who runs the dress-and-notions shop, You Sew and Sew. (She is a major figure in *Needful Things*.)

We meet Ace's uncle, Reginald "Pop" Merrill, who runs an antique store on Main Street, the Emporium Galorium (mentioned in "The Body"). It is Pop Merrill who, at Kevin Delevan's request, examines the Sun camera and later steals it, paying for it with his life.

A postcard published by Viking in 1991 to promote *Needful Things*, the King novel in which the fictional town of Castle Rock is destroyed when the devil decides to pay a visit.

Needful Things

> Wasn't nothing ordinary about what happened to Reginald "Pop" Merrill, either— Pop was the old miser who used to run the town junk shop. The Emporium Galorium, it was called. . . . His nephew Ace says somethin' spooky happened to his uncle before that fire—somethin' like on *The Twilight Zone*. Of course, Ace wasn't even around when his uncle bit the dust; he was finishing a four-year stretch in Shawshank Prison for breaking and entering in the nighttime.
>
> —from the narrator's introduction to *Needful Things*

The stage set, it's time, as King put it in his introduction to "The Sun Dog," to "close the book on Castle Rock, Maine, where so many of my own favorite characters have lived and died. Enough, after all, is enough. Time to move on (maybe all the way next door to Harlow, ha-ha). But I didn't want to walk away; I wanted to finish things, and do it with a bang." This 640-page novel does in fact end with a bang, just as King promises, but it begins with a whimper: as in *'Salem's Lot*, a mysterious stranger comes to town.

He's not an emissary from the devil but, in fact, is the devil himself—Satan, Old Scratch, Beelzebub—who has come to Castle Rock to give people their needful things, the things they just can't live without, for a price which seems too good to be true: a deed (or misdeed, actually) that, domino-like, will in the end topple their quiet town.

The newcomer, Leland Gaunt, through his machinations, has stirred the soup, a hellish brew of discontentment, and it's up to Sheriff Pangborn, to stop the devil himself.

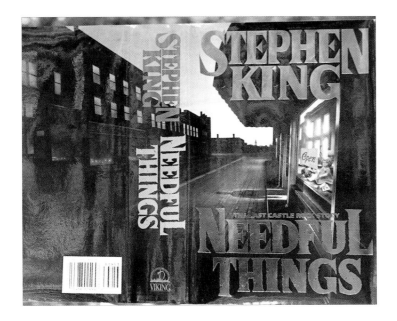

Unfortunately, Ace Merrill—like a bad penny—turns up and has devilment on his mind. "It's Miller Time," Ace announces, as he sets up the sticks of dynamite to blow up the Castle Stream Bridge, which explodes at 7:38 P.M. on October 15, 1991.

Ace and his father, however, are not through: They detonate forty sticks at the Municipal Building on Lower Main Street, killing nineteen people.

Meanwhile, in the streets, the Catholics and the Baptists are at war, as Pangborn confronts Gaunt, who escapes in his supernatural wagon. "It rose over Castle Stream, a glowing box in the sky; it passed over the downed bridge which lay in the torrent like the skeleton of a dinosaur.

"Then a raft of smoke from the burning hulk of the Municipal Building blew across Main Street, and when the smoke cleared, Leland Gaunt and his hellwagon were gone." And so was Castle Rock.

The narrator, who originally welcomed the reader to Castle Rock, reappears. This time, however, he's introducing the reader not to Castle Rock but to Junction City, Iowa, where a new store is opening. "Interesting name for a story, ain't it?" poses the narrator. "Answered Prayers. Makes you wonder what's for sale inside."

Irma Skillins, who was the principal at Junction City High School, has retired and she's checking out the new store. King writes, "If nothing else, I imagine she'll want to get a good look at whoever it was decided to put that bright red awning over Sam Peebles's old office!" (Peebles was the Junction City realtor and insurance man who lost two library books and thereby invoked the wrath of the demon wraith Ardelia Lortz, recounted in *Four Past Midnight*'s "Library Policeman.")

But, as they say, that's another story . . . for another time.

CHAPTER 5: TERRA INCOGNITA— THE ROAD WEST

As King readers know, Maine is Stephen King's main haunt, but Stephen King country can be found virtually anywhere on a map of the United States. A haunted ghost story would seem ideally suited to New England or, perhaps, New Orleans, but King set *The Shining* in Colorado, at a resort hotel high in the Rockies.

Above and opposite: A weekend jaunt to the majestic Stanley Hotel in Estes Park, Colorado inspired King to write *The Shining*. (Photo courtesy of the *Estes Park Trail-Gazette*)

And can you imagine a horrific story of human sacrifice set in the Bible belt? King did, and the result was "Children of the Corn," set in Gatlin, Nebraska, where teenagers worship a corn deity that demands bloody tribute. What about a story in which the dead come alive? In "You Know They Got a Hell of a Band," the ungrateful dead play to a captive audience in Rock and Roll Heaven, Oregon. Or what about a ghost town in what used to be called the wild west? Things are still pretty wild in some places, such as the town King writes about in *Desperation*. In the geography of King's mind, points west—far from Maine—can be just as haunting as his home state.

It was time for a change of scenery, Tabitha King said. Stephen King agreed, but neither could suggest a place. "I know how to solve this," he told her, pulling out an oversized road atlas.

He opened it up to a two-page spread of the United States, closed his eyes, and pointed to the map, to Boulder, Colorado.

In late summer 1974, the Kings moved temporarily to Boulder, where they rented a house. Nestled against the foot of the Rockies—a starkly beautiful range of snow-capped mountains that extends from north to south—Boulder seemed like a world away from the Kings' familiar haunts in Maine.

Unable to write at their rented house, King rented a room in downtown Boulder,

"A landmark. A King-sized scary story."
– ARCHER WINSTEN, NEW YORK POST

Stanley Kubrick's *The Shining* (1980) was filmed mostly at Elstree Studios, near London, not at the Stanley Hotel in Colorado, which was King's inspiration for the 1977 novel. (The façade of the hotel that appears in the movie was modeled after the Tiberland Hotel in Oregon.)

where he began work on *The House on Value Street*, which proved to be as unassailable as the mountains that surrounded him. Like a castle under siege, the book resisted King's invasive efforts. The roman à clef of the Patricia Hearst kidnapping, a plague of violence as he put it, simply refused to be written.

As it turned out, *The House on Value Street* was a trial cut for a much more ambitious book, *The Stand*, an epic story of good versus evil, with Randal Flagg—King's most memorable villain, the black magician, the walking dude—at its center.

In late October, Stephen and Tabitha decided it was time for a vacation away from the kids, since they hadn't had any private time to themselves in some years. It would be a welcome and much-needed break.

They asked around, and the locals suggested the Stanley Hotel in Estes Park, about thirty miles to the northwest as the crow flies. A grand old hotel, the Stanley sounded like the perfect getaway, so the Kings got away, only to discover that on the day they arrived, the hotel was closing down for the season.

Because winter snowstorms made the roads up to the Stanley Hotel impassable, it hibernated for the winter. So just as most of the hotel's guests were checking out, the Kings checked in.

Call it luck or serendipity, but the weekend jaunt was just what King needed to jump-start his overactive imagination, which by then was going into maximum over-drive. The spooky landscape; the almost funereal, businesslike atmosphere of the hotel staff as it went down its checklist for shutting down the hotel; the quiet hallways—all had an effect on King, as did an earlier book idea that came back to haunt him: a story about a young boy who was a psychic receptor.

This place, King knew, was the perfect setting for his genus loci—his haunted place—just as Shirley Jackson, whom he greatly admired, had explored in *The Haunting of Hill House*.

In some ways, this location was even better than Jackson's. Who knew what ghosts haunted this hotel? What of its history? Why was this hotel built here, and why?

That night at dinner, the Kings were the only guests. They sat in a cavernous dining room and listened to recorded music instead of the live band that usually played dinner music. A solemn waiter suggested beef for dinner, because that was all they had left in the oversized freezer in the hotel's kitchen.

When the Kings returned to their room, Tabitha called it a night, but Stephen's restless imagination haunted him, so he walked down to the bar, where he was served by a bartender named Grady.

At one point, as he explained in an essay on *The Shining*, he passed a coiled fire hose—a thick, cotton hose capped with a brass nozzle, carefully rolled up behind a glass enclosure. In King's mind, the hose came alive; King thought he heard it thump on the carpet of the hall . . . and the bare bones of a new novel took shape.

"Here's Johnny." Jack Nicholson as Jack Torrance in Kubrick's *The Shining*.

The story of the boy as the psychic receptor finally clicked; the boy would be named Danny Torrance, and he had a gift, the "shine." Taking its lyrics from a popular John Lennon song—"We all shine on . . . "—*The Shining* would firmly establish King as a writer of supernatural fiction. First, *Carrie*, the girl with telekinetic powers; then *'Salem's Lot*, with vampires infesting a small Maine town; and now this, a novel about a haunted hotel. It looked as if a brand name in horror was shaping itself.

In *The Shining*, Jack Torrance comes to the Overlook Hotel to redeem himself, to put his own personal ghosts behind him—his fears of inadequacy, his fits of unintentional rage, his drunken past. He would start a new life by being a model breadwinner for his small family—his wife Wendy and their son Danny.

Drawing on memories from his earlier days of what it was like to be in a similar life situation, when King was a young father living in the double-wide mobile home in Hermon, *The Shining* is not so much about the haunted hotel but the haunted man; the novel is clearly the story of a family with no center, spinning out of control. (Mirroring his own abandonment as a child, King's earlier works featured fragmented families, a stark contrast to the traditional nuclear family that he saw on TV when he was growing up, in shows like *Father Knows Best* and *Leave It to Beaver*. In *Carrie*, there is no father figure; in *'Salem's Lot*, Mark Petrie is orphaned; in "The Body," Gordon Lachance's

brother dies in a freak accident; and in *The Shining*, the father is clearly out of control.)

The Shining literally put King on the literary map: It was his first hardcover bestseller, and went on to sell spectacularly as a paperback, as *Carrie* and *'Salem's Lot* did previously.

Deliberately structured as a five-act play, *The Shining* was ideally suited for film adaptation and, after the success of *Carrie*, interest in *The Shining* was inevitable. *'Salem's Lot*, though no less powerful than *The Shining*, had a more difficult premise to portray cinematically—vampiric infestation in small-town Maine. In contrast, a movie set in a large haunted hotel perched high in the Colorado mountains was easier to imagine, a lot easier to sell to the studios, and a lot easier to film.

Stanley Kubrick took on the formidable task of translating *The Shining* to the screen. Shooting principally at a studio near London, *The Shining* proved to be—depending on whether or not you are a Kubrick fan—either a visual delight or an exercise in self-indulgence. Beautifully scored with haunting music and artfully filmed, Kubrick's *The Shining* was clearly more his vision than Stephen King's. But what Kubrick didn't, or wouldn't, acknowledge was that King fans see King-based movies to get the crap scared out of them—to be terrified, which is the finest effect horror fiction can achieve, according to King.

Though the film was hugely profitable—due in large part to the box-office draw of Jack Nicholson, who had recently won an Oscar for his stunning performance as Randal McMurphy in *One Flew Over the Cuckoo's Nest*—the film left King crestfallen. A famous director's reputation, big budgets, and star actors were no guarantees that his books would be faithfully adapted to the screen—a realization that, time and again, would continue to haunt big-budget King films.

For now, however, King kept up a stiff upper lip, and thumped the drum for the film; privately, he was disappointed, because he felt Kubrick had missed the point: the subtext of the novel was the haunted family, not the haunted hotel, which was simply the setting for Jack Torrance's slow, inevitable descent into madness.

Someday, King decided, he'd direct a remake himself. If you want to get it right, you have to do it yourself. And, in the years that followed, King complained about *The Shining* in print, as Stanley Kubrick remained offstage and took King's heat without comment.

Cut to the late nineties, by which time Stephen King had become an entertainment powerhouse, a best-selling author with a long string of film and television adaptations made from his works. Although the film adaptations had been a mixed bag—ranging from King's self-directed, self-termed "moron movie" (*Maximum Overdrive*) to the brilliant *Stand By Me* and *The Shawshank Redemption*—the TV adaptations had fared much better.

Opposite: The facade of the Stanley, made to resemble the Overlook in preparation for the filming of *Stephen King's The Shining*. (Photo courtesy of the *Estes Park Trail-Gazette*)

Stephen King in a cameo as the bandleader of the Gage Creed Band in ABC-TV's *The Shining*. (Photo courtesy of the *Estes Park Trail-Gazette*)

In fact, King realized, if he could persuade ABC-TV to let him do *The Shining* as a miniseries, the format would allow the intricate novel the room it needed to breathe, to come to life.

ABC, which saw the value of new wine from an old bottle, so to speak, gave a green light to the project based on King's script—presumably the same one, perhaps updated, that he had given to Kubrick, who rejected it in favor of his own script. But one stumbling block remained: It required the permission of the studio . . . and Kubrick.

All the birds came home to roost. Mindful of the many criticisms King made about *The Shining*—cutting comments that, over the years, had become increasingly vocal as King gave numerous interviews to the media—Kubrick set as his condition of consent that King not make any further comments to the media about the original version of *The Shining*. King acquiesced and *Stephen King's The Shining* went forward.

This time, however, the director, Mick Garris, decided to return to the geographic roots of the story. Despite the disclaimer that appears in the front of the novel, it is clear that the Stanley Hotel was in fact the inspiration for the Overlook, so Garris went to Estes Park, Colorado, to soak up the atmosphere and see if the miniseries could be filmed on location, instead of using a film stage merely gussied up to resemble a haunted hotel. Garris, in short, wanted to film the genuine article.

The Shining Ale, No. 217 and Redrum Ale were brewed exclusively for the Stanley Hotel by the Estes Park Brewery.

Despite the encroachment of the nearby town, which required artful composition to give the illusion that the hotel itself was truly isolated, the sample footage suggested that *Stephen King's The Shining* could be filmed on location. (In truth, if the Torrances had been trapped in the real-world

Estes Park hotel during a blizzard, all they'd have to do is leave the hotel and walk down the street to any of the stores that had sprung up in the interim since the Kings' visit in 1974.)

The end result: a version of *The Shining* that pleased the critics, the King fans, the television studio, and King. One of his finest novels, *The Shining* was now caught on film the way the author intended, due in large part to his having written the script and co-produced the miniseries. (He also appears in a cameo, as the band director of the Gage Creed band—his way of saying: Hey, I'm going to mix business with pleasure!)

Behind the scenes during the production of *Stephen King's The Shining*, which aired in 1997 on ABC-TV. (Photo courtesy of *Estes Park Trail-Gazette*)

Blessed with an outstanding cast—Steven Weber as Jack Torrance, Rebecca De Mornay as his wife Wendy, and Courtland Mead as their son Danny—the book finally gets the adaptation it so richly deserves; and on this remake, King has no cause for complaint.

Interestingly, the hotel that used to close for the winter is now open year-round and offers different lodging packages, including one they call "The Shining," which includes accommodations and souvenirs. (Do you think that includes a bloody mallet?)

But if you go to the Stanley, remember this: If you're walking down the hall and pass a firehose, and you hear something—maybe the firehose—thump on the carpet, just keep walking and don't look back.

GATLIN, NEBRASKA

Let's head further west to another admittedly spooky part of the country—the desolate corn fields of Nebraska, where King set "Children of the Corn," a short story written in 1978, collected in *Night Shift*, and adapted as a movie in 1984. Here the harvest moon seems bloated, almost too life-sized, as it shines down on the rustling rows of stalks . . . harboring who knows what?

King imagined a town named Gatlin, Nebraska, where Burt and Vicky Robeson are, as usual, at each other's throats. Setting out from Boston on a coast-to-coast drive in a last-ditch effort to save their failing marriage, the Robeson's verbal sniping distracts them from what they should have seen through the windshield—a body on the road.

The car thumps after hitting the body, and both Burt and Vicky are deathly afraid that their own private war has claimed a casualty. But when they cautiously take a closer look, they discover that Burt didn't kill the boy. His throat cut, the boy was dead before they showed up.

John Franklin is the actor who plays Isaac, leader of a cult of Nebraskan youths in *Children of the Corn* (1984).

In Gatlin, Nebraska, where the population used to be 5,431 (according to the town's welcome sign), the current population is now far less because there are no adults still living. Only a handful of souls remain.

In Gatlin, it is as if time froze in August 1964—the last month showing on a calendar in a long-deserted bar—and instead of worshipping God, the youths worship a corn deity, "He Who Walks Behind the Rows."

The teenagers have the run of the town and, needing sacrifices, providentially find the Robesons.

ROCK AND ROLL HEAVEN, OREGON

Further to the west, another couple on a roadtrip—this time a happily married couple—are leaving Portland, Oregon, and heading south. Like the Robesons, they too are unwittingly heading for King country. Their story, "You Know They Got a Hell of a Band" is collected in *Nightmares & Dreamscapes* (1993).

After spending the night in a town west of Eugene, Oregon, Mary and Clark head southeast on Route 58, then hit Route 97, with the intention of heading south to Klamath Falls, a town not far from the California state line. But when they stop for lunch in Oakridge, Clark suggests they get off Route 58 to bypass the heavy traffic. The plan, he says, is to get on State Route 42, then drive through Toketee Falls, and over to U.S. Route 97. (In actuality, there's no SR 42, and no Toketee Falls in Oregon, but there is a Forest Road 42.)

Didn't anyone tell Clark that haste makes waste?

The route he's planning will take them through a desolate part of the Cascade Range, parts of which are closed off for the winter. On the map, the word "wilderness" appears with predictable frequency throughout the entire Cascade Range, and it's not a misprint.

They set off and are soon lost after turning off of SR 42 and onto the dirt road that's supposed to be a straight shot to Toketee Falls. Instead, it's a straight shot to hell, in the guise of a town called Rock and Roll Heaven.

On the surface the town appears normal, but Mary and Clark's sense of disquiet mounts, and Mary's instincts tell her that they should turn around. Still they continue, driving down Main Street, and find themselves in what King terms "the Peculiar Little Town people kept stumbling into in various episodes of *The Twilight Zone*."

Everything in the town recalls rock-and-roll iconography. They pass the White Rabbit (a pet shop) and stop at The Rock-a-Boogie-Restaurant, where the waitress, a redhead, has an oddly familiar voice. The jukebox is filled with music from the fifties, and everything on the menu is appropriately named—Hound Dog (for a hot dog), Chubby Checker (a cheeseburger), and a Big Bopper (double cheeseburger). Mary finally recognizes the raspy, unmistakable voice of the waitress, and she realizes she's seeing the spitting image of Janis Joplin. The cook is Ricky Nelson. And the mayor? Who else but Elvis Presley.

They are far off the beaten track and, like others who were unfortunate enough to find their way here, find themselves in a timeless town where the band plays to rock the dead every night, where the hapless visitors are the captive audience because their luck hit rock bottom, and for the remainder of their lives—what's left of it, anyway—they'll experience, again and again, rock-and-roll heaven . . . or, actually, hell, because like the apparitions that haunt this town, rock and roll will never die.

DESPERATION, NEVADA

On the Automobile Association of America's 1997 map of Nevada, the text points out that "twenty minutes from the clinking coins of Reno and Las Vegas, the only sound is wind whisking across seemingly endless miles of sagebrush" and "the skeletal buildings of abandoned mining towns stare back at their boom-and-bust yesterdays."

Bisecting Nevada from west to east, Route 50 is perhaps one of the most desolate roads in the United States. For hundreds of miles, there's precious little to see, except the aforementioned hulks of the mining towns. In short, there's no more gold in them thar hills . . . but King manages to mine Desperation, an imaginary town.

King, driving his daughter Naomi's car back from Reed College in Oregon, was traveling on Route 50 in Nevada, when he passed through a small town curiously devoid of people. What, King thought, happened here?

King's imaginative answer to that question can be found in *Desperation*, a novel published in 1996.

Millions of readers have paid vicarious visits to rural Maine through King's spine-chilling novels, but Pet Sematary *is the first movie adaptation to be filmed in the author's home state.*

—Jerry Harkavy, Associated Press writer, in the *Bangor Daily News* (April 26, 1989)

She has the power to set objects afire
with just one glance.

It's a power she does not want.
It's a power she cannot control.
And, each night, Charlie prays
to be just like every other child.

But there are those who will do
everything in their power
to find her, control her . . .
or destroy her.

Charlie McGee is Stephen King's

FIRESTARTER

Will she have the power...to survive?

DINO DE LAURENTIIS presents
"FIRESTARTER"
Starring in Order of Appearance DAVID KEITH · DREW BARRYMORE
FREDDIE JONES · HEATHER LOCKLEAR · MARTIN SHEEN
GEORGE C. SCOTT · ART CARNEY · LOUISE FLETCHER
Screenplay by STANLEY MANN Based on the Novel by STEPHEN KING Music by TANGERINE DREAM
Associate Producer MARTHA SCHUMACHER Produced by FRANK CAPRA Jr. Directed by MARK L. LESTER
READ THE SIGNET BOOK · SOUNDTRACK AVAILABLE ON MCA RECORDS AND CASSETTES © 1984 Universal City Studios, Inc. · A UNIVERSAL RELEASE · R RESTRICTED

stephen king's Sometimes dead is better
PET SEMATARY

BASED ON THE BEST SELLING THRILLER

PARAMOUNT PICTURES PRESENTS A RICHARD P. RUBINSTEIN PRODUCTION A MARY LAMBERT FILM "PET SEMATARY" ELLIOT GOLDENTHAL
starring MICHAEL GWILYM DENISE CROSBY screenplay by PETER WELLER Director of Photography MITCHELL KLAUS Edited by TOM ZIMMERMAN screenplay by STEPHEN KING
Produced by RICHARD P. RUBINSTEIN Directed by MARY LAMBERT R RESTRICTED A PARAMOUNT PICTURE

CHAPTER 6: SILVER SCREAMS—MAKING
MOVIES IN STEPHEN KING'S MAINE

Previous page: Drew Barrymore and Stephen King pose outside the King home in Bangor before attending the locally held world premiere of *Firestarter* (1984). (Photo courtesy of the *Bangor Daily News*) Above: *Firestarter* premiered in Maine, but *Pet Sematary* (1989)—as a condition of the sale of the book's movie rights—was an all-Maine production.

Ten-year-old Stephen King was at a theater in Stratford, Connecticut, when " . . . the terror—the real terror, as opposed to whatever demons and boogeys which might have been living in my own mind—began on an afternoon in October of 1957," he writes in *Danse Macabre*.

He was watching *Earth vs. the Flying Saucers* when, in the middle of the movie, the projector turned off and the lights went up. A manager stood on the stage and announced that the Russians had launched Sputnik, the first satellite to orbit the Earth.

A baby boomer who grew up in the atomic age, King realized, even then, the implications of a Russian satellite. As King wrote, "For me, it was the end of the sweet dream . . . and the beginning of the nightmare."

Suddenly, the ominous warnings voiced in *Earth vs. the Flying Saucers* took on a new reality. "Look to your skies . . . a warning will come from your skies . . . look to your skies. . . ."

Gorging himself on popular culture—the science fiction movies of his time, television shows like *The Outer Limits* and *The Twilight Zone*, monster magazines, pulp fiction, and radio dramatizations like Arch Obler's *Lights Out*—King's writing style was not so much influenced by the prose style of literature but by the oral tradition of story-telling and the cinema. (This is why, when he signs a copy of *Night Shift*, he compares the stories to short films, inscribing: "Hope you enjoy these one-reelers.")

King's lifelong love affair with the movies continued when his mother moved the family to Durham, where King spent Saturdays at the movie theater in nearby Lisbon Falls. By then, he had grown to six feet and had to bring his birth certificate to prove he still qualified for a child's ticket.

Not surprisingly, years later when King began publishing, Hollywood came knocking. Though some people thought it was a fluke that *Carrie*—King's first published novel—was adapted to the screen, in retrospect it's easy to see why: King's emphasis is on story, on the people, and is told in a straightforward plot. Because his stories play well in what King calls "skull cinema," they are tailor-made for film or television adaptations.

Ironically, although King has had more of his works adapted to the visual medium than any other contemporary writer, few had been made in his home state of Maine, which always rankled King.

The problem, he knew, was twofold: first, Hollywood prefers to shoot in its own backyard, because location shooting is expensive, time-consuming, and problematic—too many things can go wrong. Those concerns are even more aggravated when you've got to shoot in a state like Maine, which has only two major jetports and—let's face it—has had for many years a backward attitude toward the film industry.

After seeing book after book of his being filmed anywhere but Maine, King felt frustrated knowing the world of difference between shooting a scene and saying it's Maine and shooting the same scene in Maine. He also knew that although Maine—like every other state—pumps a lot of money into promoting itself to tourists, it never made the connection that film work helps sell the state worldwide, for free. Finally, King noted, the film industry is a clean one; it comes in, sets up, spends its money, and leaves no trace of its presence, except for the infusion of cash—a lot of it, usually in small communities that can use the money.

In 1981, King persuaded the producer of *Creepshow* to give Maine a look-see. As the *Bangor Daily News* reported, "The location scout found a stretch of beach he liked in Ogonquit. But when he went to a town official to ask that it be cordoned off for shooting, the selectman said firmly, 'We can't do that.'" When asked why, he replied, "Because we never have." As a result, small businesses in Ogonquit lost out on an estimated $80,000, and the sequence, "Something to Tide You Over," was shot elsewhere.

King likely shook his head in frustration. Unfortunately, at the time, he could expect no help from the Maine Film Commission—it didn't exist. Unlike all the other states with an active film commission, Maine was far behind the times.

King, quoted in the *Bangor Daily News*, explained that "In Maine, there's all this talk about developing new businesses, but no one thinks of the film industry. The film community says, 'We can't shoot in Maine. We'd be too far away from our technical facilities in Los Angeles.' But they haven't thought of the technical facilities in New York. . . . Film is a clean industry. But towns are skeptical if it hasn't been done there before."

The loss of $80,000 to the Ogonquit businesses should have been a lesson learned, because the next time Maine lost out, the stakes might be a lot higher—a major motion picture that would mean a substantial loss of revenue to the small businesses in the state if Hollywood shot elsewhere.

The point was reinforced when Maine lost out to New Hampshire for *On Golden Pond*, starring Henry Fonda and his daughter, Jane. Millions of dollars were pumped into the small towns in nearby New Hampshire—Maine got nothing. Clearly, someone would have to bridge the gap between Hollywood and the state of Maine, and that person was Stephen King.

Though *Creepshow* never saw on-location shooting in Maine, King ensured that a segment from *Creepshow 2*, "The Hitchhiker," would in part be shot in Maine, giving him the ammunition needed to take on the state, which had a laissez-faire attitude toward on-location film production within its borders.

The infusion of cash and the fact that the film community cleaned up after itself, restoring the location sites to their original states, was proof enough to the citizens of Brewer, who saw the segment shoot on the nearby I-365 extension and were glad to see Hollywood come and go.

Creepshow (1982) was not filmed in Maine, but King's insistence that a segment of *Creepshow 2* (1987) be shot in his home state helped lead to the creation of a Maine Film Commission.

At a reception hosted by Laurel (the company that produced *Creepshow 2*) at the Maine Center of the Arts, King and a Maine film producer beat the drums to rally support for the state to allocate funds for a real film commission, not the makeshift one that then existed and that King characterized as "a phone in an empty office."

Henry Nevison, a former UM film producer who served as the location manager for *Creepshow 2*, told the crowd that he had been "trying to get the film commission going for some time," but his pleas fell on deaf ears. But now, with proof positive—the money from *Creepshow 2*—and

King's hammering, buttressed by Laurel producer Richard Rubenstein who echoed King's comments, the fact was undeniable: Now was the time for the legislature to budget for a state film commission.

King later carried his argument to the state legislature. As the *Bangor Daily News* reported, King "described how millions of dollars in film production money is slipping through the state's grasp because it makes no effort to encourage moviemakers to shoot in Maine."

King argued persuasively for the proposed $140,000 two-year budget to fund the new film commission, as did the sponsor of the bill, House Majority Leader John N. Diamond (D-Bangor), who said moviemaking was an "attractive, non-polluting and lucrative industry, one that generates income and employment without depleting natural resources. . . . It seems strange that Maine, with its heavy economic dependence on tourism, is the only state in the country that does not spend money to cultivate this industry." A convinced legislature allocated the money, and Lea Girardin was named as the director of the Maine Film Commission.

The novel *Cujo* is set in New England, but the 1983 film was shot in northern California in a town called "Little New England."

Girardin makes no bones about King's role in the establishment of the commission. "Maine owes Stephen King a lot," she told the *Bangor Daily News*. "He's done much to bring these types of activities and related benefits to the state. My job," she added, "is to bring people into the state to make films, commercials or any kind of production, and to make it easy and successful so they'll want to come back or spread the word that Maine is a good place to film."

No longer would King's movies have to be shot in northern California, in a town called "Little New England" because of its uncanny resemblance to the original. But, as King pointed out to the *Bangor Daily News*, "It looks like New England if it's set in Maine. It'll be more authentic, and a new look. *Cujo* was shot in a northern California town that looked like New England, but the ocean was always on the wrong side of the screen."

When it came time to film *Pet Sematary*, which promised to be one of the biggest grossing King films, he didn't want to leave anything to chance. As a condition of its sale, it had to be made in Maine. Shot entirely in Maine, from first frame to last, *Pet Sematary* drew on a lot of Maine resources:

·The film was largely shot in Hancock County.

·Dozens of extras were hired from the Greater Bangor area.

·The Bangor International Airport was transformed into Boston's Logan Airport for one of the shots.

·In Ellsworth, the "pet sematary" was re-created, looking—if anything—more real and more spooky than the actual cemetery. (Now there's movie magic for you!)

·Betty and Charles Lewis saw their two homes on West Side Road leased to the production company. (Betty Lewis was blasé about all the movie excitement that characterized most of the townfolk. "I don't get ga-ga over movie stars," she told the hometown newspaper. "Stephen King was in my kitchen the other day, and I didn't drop dead. It didn't excite me.")

·Mount Hope Cemetery was the site of Gage Creed's memorial service, with Stephen King in a cameo role as the preacher.

·The Bangor State Armory was, for eight weeks, transformed into a set for indoor shooting. Mike Policare, a representative of Paramount Pictures, which distributed the film, spoke appreciatively of the National Guard's hospitality. In the *Bangor Daily News*, Policare said, "Basically we were given free rein of the armory. We needed a soundstage suitable for production, and the armory was the only building in the area with the right design. It offered controlled access, plenty of room and storage, dressing rooms, parking and utilities."

Breaking from tradition, Paramount—for the first time in its history—scheduled Bangor for a promotional screening, an event usually restricted to the top fifty markets.

Anyone who read *Pet Sematary* knew what to expect. The film is clearly more gory than most of King's books, which should come as no surprise because of the subject matter, but those who attended the promotional screenings prior to the film's official release date of April 21, 1989, found much to like in this all-Maine production.

Stephen King's Graveyard Shift (1990), shot entirely in Maine, shows a gritty side of the state that tourists never see.

The *Bangor Daily News* interviewed several moviegoers as they emerged from the theater after a screening. Perry Boudreau said, "I had read the book and really liked it. The film followed the book really well. It had enough suspense to keep you on the edge of your seat, even if you knew what was going to happen next." Tim Cameron observed, "A lot of it was made in Ellsworth. It was nice and gory. That's why I went to see it." As for King himself, even before he saw the finished film, he saw the design drawings and said, "Look, I've got goosebumps."

THE STORM OF THE CENTURY

The ABC-TV miniseries *The Storm of the Century*, from Rainfall Productions, airs in the spring of 1999. Based on King's original three-hundred-page script, and budgeted at $35 million, the plot, writes Lois R. Shea of the *Boston Globe*, seems straightforward: "A raging blizzard hits a small town, communications with the outside world are cut, and a mysterious stranger shows up who happens to be the embodiment of pure evil. Mayhem ensues."

Sounds like a mixture of the plot elements from *The Shining* and *Needful Things*, but let's give King the benefit of the doubt. After all, his remake of *The Shining* was top-notch. (Note: In *The Shining* miniseries, *Wings* actor Steven Weber starred in the lead role. In *The Storm of the Century*, fellow *Wings* actor Tim Daly plays the lead role. Daly told the *Boston Globe* about the miniseries: "It's about integrity and it's about the price you pay for losing your integrity—and, more interestingly, the price you pay for keeping your integrity.")

Still sounds like *Needful Things* to me. . . .

For its Maine shots, the production is on-location in Southwest Harbor, which is a small town, even by Maine standards. Writes Shea, "Two thousand people live here year round, and winter generally finds them building and repairing boats, shrimping, diving for sea urchins, and preparing bed and breakfasts for the onslaught of summer." The shoot, notes Shea, will pump "at least $1 million into the local economy."

MAXIMUM OVERDRIVE

A movie-by-movie explication of every King film is beyond the scope of this book—for that, consult one of the four books on the subject—but *Maximum Overdrive* bears mention here, if only because of King's extensive involvement and because it required, for the duration of the on-location shoot, King's presence in Wilmington, North Carolina.

In trailers promoting the film, Stephen King addresses the movie-going audience, saying: "Y'know, a lot of people have made movies out of my stories . . . but I thought it was time I took a crack at doing Stephen King . . . After all, if you want it done right, you have to do it yourself."

The project: a feature-length film based on "Trucks," a one-note King story collected in *Night Shift*, based on an original screenplay by King, and directed by King.

Triple insurance, wouldn't you say?

Filmed at the edge of a highway ten miles away from Wilmington, *Maximum Overdrive* required the construction of a truck stop, a set so real that truckers pulled off the road, wanting to get their tanks topped off and to grab a burger at the Dixie Boy Truck Stop diner.

From July to October 1985, King gave himself a crash course on filmmaking, from the director's chair. Sweltering in the summer heat near the coastal town whose claim to fame is that basketball legend Michael Jordan grew up there, King spent up to fourteen hours a day working on location, setting up shots, and reviewing the dailies (the unedited footage). He spent evenings working on *IT* at the rented house that— temporarily—he called home.

As for the film itself, let's keep in mind that it was, after all, King's directorial debut. (He even made a cameo appearance in the beginning of the film, in which he's insulted by an ATM machine.) So let's not judge the movie too harshly. In fact, let's be charitable and admit that it was a learning experience for King, who left that summer to head home with a newfound appreciation of how unbelievably difficult it is to make a good film, after years of criticizing directors and producers who, like him, tried their best but failed to deliver a crowd-and critic-pleasing film.

AFTERWORD

Here I am, where I ought to be. A writer must have a place where he or she feels this, a place to love and be irritated with. . . . Location, whether it is to abandon or to draw it sharply, is where we start.

—Louise Erdrich, *The New York Times Book Review*, July 28, 1995

For Stephen King, Maine is where his fiction starts and ends. In his fictional landscapes, in Maine towns like Chamberlain, Ludlow, Haven, Derry, and most especially Castle Rock, we see Maine through native eyes. We feel the pulse of these towns—each with its own distinctive beat—and through the fiction, we see what lies just below the surface. We discover that we are seeing a microcosm of our world, no matter where we may live.

A writer's sense of place is the geographic center of the writer's imaginary landscape. Drawing from the real world, writing about an imaginary world, Stephen King has laid claim to Maine in the same way that Steinbeck claimed Salinas Valley, in the same way that Faulkner claimed Yoknapatawpha County.

King has put his unmistakable mark on the fictional landscape of Maine, and in doing so has earned himself a place not only as a regional writer but as a popular writer. In recent years he has acquired a growing and long overdue reputation as a writer who is justifiably praised by the likes of Joyce Carol Oates and others who see the writer—not the boogeyman, as he was promoted by his early publishers.

For King readers who want to better understand his work, a trip to Maine is indispensable. However, because it's not practical for many readers—Maine is, after all, off the beaten track—this book gives you a glimpse of the world in which King lives and of the fictional world that comprises the landscape of his imagination. It is this intersection of the real and the unreal that makes his stories uniquely, and entertainingly, his own.

Keeping up with King's output—and those of his chroniclers—is no easy task, especially for the new King reader.

Because there's a wealth of material in print by and about King, I'm keeping my recommendations on the short side.

BOOKS BY GEORGE BEAHM

Stephen King Country is my fifth book about Stephen King. Of those books, here's what's in print:

The Stephen King Companion (1995), from Andrews McMeel. This is, like its predecessor (published in 1989) a resource and reference guide, with articles, profiles, interview material, and sidebars about King's life and work.

Stephen King: America's Best-Loved Boogeyman (1998), from Andrews McMeel. This is not merely a revised and updated version of my previous biography on King, *The Stephen King Story*, but is in fact a brand new book, current through early 1998.

Stephen King from A to Z: An Encyclopedia of His Life and Work (1998), from Andrews McMeel. With twenty-six illuminated letters by artist Stephen Fabian, dozens of photos (including book-jacket covers), a dozen essays on topics concerning things King, and hundreds of entries covering his life and work in detail, this book covers the nooks and crannies that went unexplored in *Companion* and *Boogeyman*.

In the works:

Stephen King Collectibles: A Price Guide, which will have hundreds of photographs of rare first editions, signed editions, and other collectibles, with prices determined by leading book dealers that specialize in the literature of the fantastic. Unlike the previous books cited above, this one is a specialty item and not generally available through bookstores. It's a small press book, from my own GB Ink, and the print run will be limited. I can be reached by snail mail at: GB Ink, PO Box 3602, Williamsburg, VA 23187.

PHANTASMAGORIA: AN UNOFFICIAL STEPHEN KING ZINE

Because the books are difficult to update, I publish a quarterly newsletter, *Phantasmagoria*, which is up to sixteen pages, depending on how much news is fit to print. Tabloid size, the zine covers King's professional activities: forthcoming books, limited editions, public appearances, and movie deals, as well as photographs, reprinted articles (from publications my readers would likely not have read), and newspaper profiles about King.

I want to stress that although it's supposed to be a quarterly publication, its frequency of publication does in fact vary, depending on what's going on in Stephen's kingdom, and the other projects that command my attention (usually books).

Mailed bulk rate or by first class, this zine is available only by direct subscription from me. Inquire for current subscription rates.

The other advantage of subscribing: I send out supplemental postcard mailings by first class, informing subscribers about the imminent release of a forthcoming King limited-edition book. (As long time subscribers know, time is of the essence, since word gets out on the Web quickly, and any King limited edition will be vastly oversubscribed and soon escalate rapidly in value. Case in point: King's self-published *Six Stories*, issued at $80, is now selling for $400—for a book published in 1997! Subscribers got the early word through a postcard mailing from me, and most of them got a copy for $80.)

As one subscriber put it, the postcard alerts are worth the price of admission to the zine.

E-MAIL

I get a good bit of e-mail, usually arriving in bunches. Typically, after an issue of *Phantasmagoria* comes out, there's a lot of e-mail.

Although I read the e-mail daily, I usually wait until the weekend to answer it, so please keep that in mind. (It's a one-person operation around here, folks.)

I'm on America Online, at Geobeahm, and my Internet e-mail address is *Geobeahm@aol.com*.

WEBSITES

I make a good-faith effort to try and keep my website updated monthly, or updated every two months, but it's a losing battle. Still, if you want more information on what's going on at GB Ink, check the website at *http://members.aol.com/geobeahm/index.html*.

Obviously, there are plenty of other websites devoted to King, but the URL's change frequently, so your best bet is to search for "Stephen King" or go to Betts Bookstore's website, where they maintain links to the other King websites worth viewing. (I plan on posting these on my website as well, so be sure to check both mine and Betts Bookstore's sites.)

BETTS BOOKSTORE

I am happy to recommend Betts Bookstore, run by Penney and Stuart Tinker, providentially located in downtown Bangor.

Betts issues an infrequent newsletter—a price list, actually, of new acquisitions for resale, plus whatever news is fit to print—but you can also call them at (207) 947-7052. Or you can e-mail them on AOL at Bettsbooks. (If you want to write them, contact: Stuart Tinker, Betts Bookstore, 26 Main Street, Bangor, ME 04401.)

Their website can be found at *http://www.acadia.net/betts*.

TOURISM INFORMATION

Exploring Maine (magazine). An annual publication of the Maine Publicity Bureau, Inc., this gives a useful overview of the entire state's touring possibilities, from the south coast area to Aroostook ("The County").

Maine: Guide to Winter (magazine). An annual publication of the Maine Publicity Bureau, Inc., with a focus on winter sports—skiing, snowmobiling, ice fishing, dog-sledding, and off-slope activities.

Down East: The Magazine of Maine. A monthly, this is clearly for tourists, from an insider's viewpoint. Columns include "Inside Maine," with tips on what to do and where to eat; "Along the Waterfront," focusing on coastal activities; Calendar of Events, festivals and shows; "Homes Down East," Maine real estate; and more. $16.95 for a year subscription.

Bangor (trade paperback), Arcadia Publishing. A look at the early years of the city, compiled by Richard R. Shaw.

Bangor: Volume II—The Twentieth Century (trade paperback), Arcadia Publishing. A collection of photos of modern-day Bangor, culled from the files of the Bangor Historical Society and the *Bangor Daily News*, compiled by Richard R. Shaw.

Maine, by Charles C. Calhoun. Part of the Compass American Guides, this trade paperback is to my mind the best general guidebook on the state, with first-rate photography, imaginative layouts, and solid information. (If your budget allows only one guidebook, get this one.)

AAA Tourbook: Maine, New Hampshire, Vermont (trade paperback, free for AAA members.) A city-by-city lodging guide, with information on activities by state and historical information by city.

Woodsmen and Whigs: Historic Images of Bangor, Maine, by Abigail Ewing Zelz and Marilyn Zoidis, with photographic printing by Diane Vatne. Trade hardcover edition. The Donning Company, Publishers.

Bangor Daily News. Daily newspaper, with the largest circulation in Maine. Frequently runs photos of King, stories about him (newsworthy events), and occasionally letters to the editor by King.

MAPS

There are plenty to choose from—take your pick:

Maine, The Way Life Should Be. The Official Map and Travel Guide of the Maine Publicity Bureau, Inc., published by Hartnett House, map publishers. The most useful general map, with the state on one side, and lodging information on the backside. (Note: the inset map of Bangor is too small to be useful.)

Maine, New Hampshire, Vermont. Published by the American Automobile Association, it's not for sale; it's free for members. (The cost of an annual membership can more than be justified in the free maps and TripTiks, customized driving maps.) Useful if you want to drive around in adjacent states.

The *Maine Atlas* and *Gazetteer,* published by DeLorme. Indispensable for anyone seriously wanting to navigate Maine, this oversized paperback book is a navigator's dream. (It also has GPS grids, so if you have a GPS receiver, you can find your location to an accuracy of approximately 25 meters.)

DeLorme also publishes a standard fold-out map, The *Maine Map and Guide,* which is excellent.

For serious navigators, DeLorme publishes a street atlas on CD-ROM (for both IBM and Mac), which allows you to type in any street in the United States and have it located in seconds. (Even more marvelous, if you have a laptop computer and DeLorme's GPS receiver, you can literally see where you are at all times on the computer screen, as the software and receiver act as your own navigator. Unbelievable.)

Bangor–Brewer Street Map and Directory, published by DeLorme. Indispensable for anyone traveling to Bangor or the greater Bangor area. This full-color map covers Old Town, Orono, Veazie, Hampden, Orrington, Holden, Hermon, Glenburn, Milford, the

University of Maine, and surrounding communities. Contact DeLorme at Two DeLorme Drive, POB 298, Yarmouth, ME 04096.

AAA Map of Greater Bangor. Free for members, this map, in black-and-white, is even more detailed than the DeLorme map. This one lists more places than its competition and, as such, is more useful for King fans wanting to check out specific sites, like the Barrens.

IMPORTANT TRAVEL TIPS FOR MAINE TRAVELERS (FROM THE OFFICIAL MAP AND GUIDE)

By law, seatbelts are required to be worn.

The sales tax is 6%.

The lodging tax is 7%.

And the maximum amounts of liquor you are allowed to bring in the state are: 1 gallon of whiskey, 1 gallon of spirits (wine/liquor), and 1 case of beer.

Smoking is prohibited in all enclosed areas of places where the public is invited or allowed.

Regarding I-95, it is illegal—and a pain in the neck—to pick up hitchhiking vampires past midnight.

RECOMMENDED BOOKS ABOUT KING

King has had dozens of books written about him, but most are for the growing ranks of academe, eager to find a new writer's body of work on which to perform a biopsy.

Unless you have a real appetite for reading articles such as "The Redrum of Time: A Meditation on Francisco Goya's 'Saturn Devouring His Children' and Stephen King's *The Shining*" (Greg Weller, in *The Shining Reader*), you may want to try one of the more accessible books.

The most accessible—invaluable, actually—book about King was the first full-length study of King, and remains the best single book on the subject of King. Douglas E. Winter's *Stephen King: The Art of Darkness* was written with King's consent and cooperation. (Obviously, King can't write his own books and help others write their books about him, so he wisely drew the line years ago and, as a matter of policy, cannot assist any writer working on a book about him and his work.)

The ideal complement to Winter's book is Stephen King's *Danse Macabre*, the author's own overview of the horror field since the fifties. Informal and informative, this book covers a lot of territory and is a "must read" for anyone interested in the genre that spawned the Boogeyman from Bangor.

If you've a mind to check out the other books about King, please consult my *Stephen King from A to Z*, which lists the contents for every book about King, with a write-up explaining the book's merits (or lack thereof).

As for books by Stephen King: For short fiction: Try *Night Shift*. It's prime King. For novellas, "The Mist" can be found in *Skeleton Crew* (his second short-fiction collection), and *Different Seasons* offers four outstanding novellas. (If you think King only writes horror, you're in for a pleasant surprise.) For novels: *'Salem's Lot*, *The Shining*, *The Stand* (either edition), *The Dead Zone*, *The Eyes of the Dragon*, *IT*, *Dolores Claiborne*, *The Green Mile*, and *Bag of Bones*. Though he's obviously written dozens more, these are a representative sampling, and will suggest other novels in their reading.

Note: All of King's books are in print, with one notable exception: *Six Stories*, his self-published book. (Those stories, however, will likely see publication in the next short-fiction collection, so don't despair for missing out on that one.)

No matter where you begin reading King's canon, one thing is certain: You will get hooked. You will want to read all the novels, all the short fiction, and even the nonfiction. King's words have that effect. He's a storyteller, and to my mind, one of the best in the trade.

Happy haunting!